THE
BIGGEST BOOK OF
YouTube
VIDEOS EVER!

First published in Great Britain in 2016
by Carlton Books
20 Mortimer Street
London W1T 3JW

A CIP catalogue for this book is available
from the British Library.

ISBN 978-1-78097-878-9

Printed and bound by CPI Group (UK) Ltd, Croydon CR0 4YY

10 9 8 7 6 5 4 3 2 1

THE
BIGGEST BOOK OF
YouTube
VIDEOS EVER!

Your guide to the coolest, craziest and funniest internet clips

CARLTON
BOOKS

"I'm sure if Shakespeare were alive today, he'd be doing classic guitar solos on YouTube."

Peter Capaldi

INTRODUCTION

Despite celebrating its eleventh birthday in February 2016, YouTube continues to be the world's favourite internet site. With over 300 hours of video uploaded every minute, there is something to suit every interest. Music, comedy, cats and dogs remain incredibly popular, but many just love the never-ending supply of weird, hilarious, jaw-dropping, surreal and completely awesome clips. It's no wonder there are a billion individual users visiting the site each month!

The selection in this book points you towards the videos that have made the news, gone super-viral or which are so good that people just return again and again to view them. You can see recent hits such as the Mutant Giant Spider Dog, the Sia Chandelier Parody, the Devil Baby Attack and the Zombie Rooftop Chase as well as YouTube favourites that include Honest Movie Trailers, Bad Lip Reading, The Slo-Mo Guys and People Are Awesome. And, of course, there are hilarious funnies, epic pranks, musical mash-ups, cute pets and loads, loads more.

"I go on YouTube when somebody
says to look something up."

George Clooney

INAPPROPRIATE LANGUAGE WARNING

The videos selected in this book do not contain any scenes of an explicit sexual or extremely gross nature. However, there is the occasional use of bad language, which is sometimes part of the video's humour. The comments sections of many of the clips often contain unnecessarily offensive, puerile and abusive language. They rarely feature any remarks of value and are generally worth switching off or ignoring.

DON'T TRY THIS AT HOME

Some of the book's clips feature stunts performed either by professionals or under the supervision of professionals. Accordingly the publishers must insist that no one attempt to re-create or re-enact any stunt or activity performed on the featured videos.

"YouTube: providing a safe home for piano-playing cats, celeb goof-ups, and overzealous lip-synchers since 2005."

Entertainment Weekly

HOW TO VIEW THE CLIPS

Each entry is accompanied by a QR code, which you can scan with your iPad or iPod. Alternatively, there is a short URL address, which you can type into your own computer, tablet or phone. Unfortunately, many of the clips are preceded by adverts, which can often be skipped after a few seconds or you may wish to download a reputable advert blocker to prevent them appearing.

CONTENTS

29

"YouTube is a place for people to share their ideas.
If by people you mean 13-year-old girls and by ideas
you mean how they love the Jonas Brothers."

Bo Burnham

THE
BIGGEST BOOK OF
YouTube
VIDEOS EVER!

IF HITCHCOCK HAD CAST RODENTS...

Suspense, mystery and small furry animals – all in five seconds

It does last just five seconds, but it has proved to be one of YouTube's greatest ever hits. Although officially called *Dramatic Chipmunk*, the rodent superstar is actually a prairie dog. The clip originally came from a Japanese television show called *Hello! Maquis Morning* in which the critter appeared in a transparent box. This would remain pretty unremarkable footage if not for the magic ingredient – three portentous chords and a rumble of thunder, taken from the soundtrack of Mel Brooks's movie *Young Frankenstein*.

http://y2u.be/a1Y73sPHKxw

THE GLOBETROTTER BOPPER

Matt dances his way around the world

Matt Harding is a great YouTube celebrity. Back in 2005, after
travelling the globe, he put together a video consisting entirely
of short clips of himself doing a silly dance in famous locations
around the world. The video, with its infectious feel-good
factor, soon racked up the hits, and Matt made more and more,
including dancing underwater and in zero-gravity conditions.
This 2012 effort was described by the *New York Times* as
"a masterpiece" and it's hard to argue with the great moves,
joyous community spirit and simply fabulous pay-off.

http://y2u.be/Pwe-pA6TaZk

A REAL BLAST

The slow-motion exploding melon

Thank heaven for the Slo Mo Guys. How else would we fill an empty few minutes if not for Gav and Dan's entertaining and sometimes educational videos? These guys make wonderful action films from inanimate objects. On their channel you'll find a wealth of fascinating "experiments", from paint explosions and flame-throwing to a sledgehammer taking on an Xbox 360 – all in glorious HD slow motion. This one is a real favourite. They wrap rubber bands around a melon until the whole thing bursts apart, splattering everywhere like something out of a Tarantino movie. Superb.

http://y2u.be/PK8dsAeMmPk

CREATURE EATER

How animals eat their food – a demonstration

Many YouTube clips are informative and educational. Don't be taken in by the title of this clip, though. *How Animals Eat Their Food* is not one of them. It is, however, a perfect example of how a simple idea can go stupidly viral and an almost flawless lesson in how to play the straight man against all the odds. Some think this is the funniest thing since their teacher accidentally farted in class, while others are left wondering what the fuss is all about. Let's leave that to your own impeccable judgement.

http://y2u.be/qnydFmqHuVo

TURTALLY OUT-THERE

This zombie knows what he likes...

When 10-year-old Jonathan Ware set off for the Rose Festival in Portland, Oregon he had little idea he was on his way to becoming a YouTube celebrity. Even when he was approached by an enthusiastic local TV reporter as he left the face-paint booth made up as a reasonably impressive zombie, everything was normal. But with a suitable chilling stare this one interview changed everything. Within hours his TV appearance had been posted online, within days parodies and remixes began to appear and within weeks Jonathan was starring on T-shirts and ringtones. It took just three little words...

http://y2u.be/CMNry4PE93Y

PLAY IT AGAIN, KITTY

Pray silence for the legendary Keyboard Cat

A cat named Fatso tinkling the old ivories … puts you in mind of some smoky jazz joint in the 1920s, doesn't it? But this Fatso is a 1980s moggie and a twenty-first-century phenomenon. Charles Schmidt filmed his keyboard-playing cat in 1984 on VHS only for it to find its way on to YouTube over 20 years later. From there, the cat's soundtrack was used on tons of epic fail videos with the title *Play him off, Keyboard Cat* – and Fatso became a hero. Unfortunately, Fatso never knew his fame; reportedly, he went to kitty heaven in 1987.

http://y2u.be/J---aiyznGQ

TEXAS CHAINSAW HEDGE MASSACRE

The World's Strongest Redneck – living life on the hedge

One day the Darwin Awards (for idiots who protect the human gene pool by making the ultimate sacrifice of their own lives) might just feature Steve McGranahan, the self-styled World's Strongest Redneck. Steve, whose previous videos feature refrigerator wrestling, piano-smashing and lawnmower-on-a-stick, turned the stupidity dial up to 11 for this attempt to keep his privets in shape. We might say, "Don't try this at home," but, judging by the state of his hedge when he's finished, you'll reach that conclusion anyway!

http://y2u.be/dyWzk31p3lk

ONE SMALL STEP FOR YOUTUBE...

Gone with the Wind for the iPad generation

It takes some talent to produce a five-minute animation that reduces its viewers to tears, but the cosmic romance *Crater Face* achieves just that — well, according to the thousands of comments anyway. CalArts student Skyler Page's story is about an astronaut putting his own life in danger as he attempts to bring two moon rocks together. The video featured in Joshgi's YouTube No Cry Challenge, and many who mocked the idea of a love affair between two little boulders causing real grief had to swallow back their tears. Are you ready to take the test?

http://y2u.be/MnA4u9CaK7A

STAND OUT FROM THE CROWD

Hallelujah! At last a flash mob worth watching

YouTube has plenty of videos showcasing flash mobs: "People who assemble suddenly in a public place, perform an unusual and seemingly pointless act for a brief time, then quickly disperse" (Wikipedia). From Azerbaijan to Zambia, seemingly unconnected folk suddenly reveal themselves as all-singing, all-dancing public entertainers. Many are expensive corporate-sponsored affairs or just too downright predictable, but this Canadian effort ticks all the boxes with drama, surprise, decent singing, festive fun and befuddled onlookers. And over 100,000 likes says it's no flash in the pan.

http://y2u.be/SXh7JR9oKVE

RUN FOR YOUR LIFE!
IT'S A...?

In cyberspace everyone can hear you scream

Another of YouTube's sub-20-second "accidental" masterpieces, this has character, plot, mystery and laughs in the time it takes to butter a slice of toast. It could be the start of a scary alien-invasion film or an axeman-at-large slasher flick. If it's staged, this is pretty convincing, but most reckon this is from the great movie that is real life. What, you will ask, could make someone so terrified? But before you ask yourself the inevitable how, why, when and where questions, you'll be left wondering just WTF?

http://y2u.be/5JYzbzqYzm0

SKUNK ON A STICK

Because you just can't beat a simple prank…

This one's a simple and classic *Candid Camera*-style caper, which does what it says on the tin. The aim is just to surprise an unsuspecting member of the public with a furry animal on the end of a stick and see what happens. Why it's funny to see someone jump out of their skin isn't important — it just is! And the moments when the expected reaction doesn't ensue are even better. Just watch the brilliant bit with the old fella who's seen it all before.

http://y2u.be/hgQPp4n05Aw

KING FOR A DAY

For those who like their sport with a side dish of culture

The famous Metropolitan Museum of Art in New York had just put the restored Velázquez portrait of King Philip IV of Spain on display. What better way to promote it than a signing session from the king himself? Will the public fall for the authentic-looking monarch, despite his being dead for over 400 years? Will the museum staff see the funny side? If you enjoy this creative prank, you'll find YouTube has more from Improv Everywhere, a New York City-based group with an avowed aim to cause "scenes of chaos and joy in public places".

http://y2u.be/TvBbVA36y1U

MOVIE MAMMA

The Matrix retold by Mum

Sci-fi movies are pretty hard to get your head around and the 1999 multi-Oscar-winning *The Matrix* is no exception. Have you seen it? Compellingly intriguing it may be, but the plot is pretty impossible to follow. So the success of filmmaker Joe Nicolosi's mother's endearing but confused attempt to describe what happens isn't that surprising. Sci-fi nerds around the world sent this viral — but the video is charming and funny, so just who is having the last laugh?

http://y2u.be/OMf9GILXouA

GHOSTLY TUNNEL VISION

Ghostly sightings deep in a Japanese tunnel

Pssst! Wanna see a ghost? A real one, not some blurry old security-camera image? Then click through this clip from tunnels dug in the mountains of Japan during World War II. The tunnels are closed to the public, but engineers were recently sent down to test radiation levels. This film is supposedly taken by one investigator who, after seeing this shirtless apparition, probably hasn't gone back. The ghost itself would scare the living daylights out of anyone, but the whisper, in Japanese, of "I am going to kill you" would send most of us straight back up that slide.

http://y2u.be/0dG8sfaqy1A

WATCHING THE MOVIES BY NUMBERS

100 Movies, 100 Quotes, 100 Numbers – awesome!

In response to the endless 100 Best Blah Blah lists, Alonzo Mosley FBI produced this fabulous countdown from 100 to 1 using only clips of movie dialogue. Guessing when and where the quotes will appear is half the fun – you know *Star Wars* and *The Wizard of Oz* will be there, but where? *The 39 Steps* (maybe you're right) and *12 Angry Men* (wrong!)?

And, just like a real Top 100, he creates real tension for the Top 10. The *Guardian* was even moved to write, "This is why the internet was invented."

http://y2u.be/FExqG6LdWHU

THE SOUND OF SILENCE

A breathtaking performance – you could hear a pin drop

In 2004 the BBC was brave enough to broadcast a rare orchestral performance of John Cage's seminal piece *4'33"* at the Barbican Hall, led by renowned conductor Lawrence Foster. What happens? Not much, but that's not giving it away, because Cage's piece is three movements of complete silence. Whatever you think of it – as a parody, a pantomime or a brutal statement of truth about music – it's hard to deny that the performance, augmented by the usual concert-hall page-turning and coughing, is something to behold.

http://y2u.be/zY7UK-6aaNA

A LOVE THAT DARES SPEAK ITS NAME

Does the Army really have an Arts and Craft Department?

"I've a real passion for…" It's a phrase you hear a lot these days, at beauty pageants, on politics shows and CVs, but the Rainbow Sponge Lady takes the concept and hammers it to death. She loves rainbow sponges with what can only be described as a passion. After the opening, "The Army Arts and Crafts Department sent me to Korea…" the whole thing gets weirder and weirder – from, "I love a sponge that is absolutely pure," to, "Oh my gosh, wiggles!" and, "This was one night I did not sleep." Pure over-the-top unadulterated brilliance!

hhttp://y2u.be/FgecK6pUQLM

WEB OF LIES

Spiders on Drugs – a YouTube classic

We're used to the crazy experiments science throws up, such as how white mice behave in a sauna or what happens when chimps are forced to play Gran Turismo, so the idea of giving spiders mind-altering substances on the end of a cotton bud shouldn't come as too much of a surprise. How might these arthropods behave under the influence of common recreational drugs and even alcohol? The results are illuminating and will help us understand much about how humans behave after a joint and a couple of bottles of wine. Watch, learn and, most of all, laugh yourself stupid!

http://youtu.be/sHzdsFiBbFc

TWO-WHEELED TERROR

From the craziest urban cycling race in the world

Extreme sports are staple YouTube fare, but now and then something comes along that gets the couch potato's adrenaline flowing. This was the 2011 edition of Valparaiso Downhill. Mountain-bike riders in the Chilean town's annual challenge have to navigate narrow flights of stairs, ramps and sheer drops at breakneck speed. The course takes the riders just two-and-a-half minutes to negotiate, but each ride packs in more thrills than a whole season of Formula 1. Just watch this fella go — and LOOK OUT FOR THE DOG!!!

http://y2u.be/jO0VLouJFNQ

SPIDERMAN, SPIDERMAN...

With his bare hands, too

Vertigo warning! Best skip this one if heights aren't your thing. They certainly don't bother French climber Alain Robert. Spiderman, as he is known, has scaled more than 70 giant structures around the globe using only his bare hands and climbing shoes and eschewing safety devices. In February 2007, in front of 100,000 onlookers, Robert attempted to scale the 185m (607ft), 40-floor Abu Dhabi Investment Authority building. Even knowing he makes it to the top, this three-and-a-half-minute account is slightly terrifying – if you find it easy watching, just wait until he waves from the top.

http://y2u.be/m2TJ3tU8mbo

A RUN OF THE MILL VIDEO

Four men, eight treadmills – one big, big internet hit

Alternative-rock group OK GO had already had YouTube success with a cheesy dance routine to their song "A Million Ways", but their follow-up, "Here It Goes Again", became a YouTube landmark. Not only was their next music video a chart-topping online hit, it even won a Grammy. A cheaply made, single-shot affair (although it took nearly 20 takes for the band to get it right), it sees the band performing a co-ordinated dance on a bank of treadmills. It's kind of nerdy but ingenious; great fun and altogether hypnotic.

http://y2u.be/dTAAsCNK7RA

THE BOSS OF THE BUSKERS

The streets of Copenhagen

It is July 1988 and Bruce Springsteen, at the height of his powers, is in Copenhagen with his E Street Band for one of his legendary four-hour shows. Taking some time out, the Boss goes off for a stroll in the city and comes across a street musician named John "Jo Jo" Magnusson. The busker has already drawn a small crowd but, when Bruce spots and picks up a spare guitar, things get a lot more interesting and suddenly Jo Jo finds himself duetting on some classic Springsteen hits.

http://y2u.be/EQzpefkdPl0

IF YOU GO DOWN TO THE WOODS TODAY

The most chilling clip on YouTube?

YouTube is packed with people trying to freak you out with ghostly goings-on, and most can be explained by camera tricks and special effects. This video is probably no different, but there is something about its simplicity that gives you goosebumps. It's just some perfectly feasible Russian out filming his dog in the woods when he comes across something ... well, something you don't tend to see every day. If you're after an explanation read the comments – or don't if you'd rather just believe.

http://y2u.be/RLqX6s39MEU

THE FABRICATED FOUR

The Beatles live on in superb Lego animation

Lego and the Beatles: both are loved all over the world, but only YouTube can bring them together to stunning effect. Using stop-motion Lego animation, YouTuber yuuhei1987 brings us the Fab Four singing "I Saw Her Standing There". John, Paul, George and Ringo are brought to incredible Lego life, the TV-show set is ingeniously devised and, of course, the soundtrack is just perfect. Enjoy this and you'll find there are plenty of other Lego music videos available, from "Bohemian Rhapsody" to "Call Me Maybe".

http://y2u.be/_xUijgqZ-xM

PUSHING ALL THE RIGHT BUTTONS

Just another day in a quiet square in Belgium

Probably the most successful corporate-made video on YouTube, this magnificent viral ad had hit three million views in just a few days – it's now pushing 50 million. To publicize their new Belgian channel, TNT put a big red button in the middle of a quiet town square and a sign reading "Push to add drama" – and waited. Now, TNT calls itself the network that "knows drama" and, as soon as an unsuspecting chap pressed the button, all hell broke loose in the most exciting, thrilling and funny 90 seconds on the web.

http://y2u.be/316AzLYfAzw

YOU STUCK-UP, HALF-WITTED, SCRUFFY-LOOKING NERF HERDER!

The 100 Greatest Movie Insults of All Time

In perfect bite-sized chunks, every great celluloid curse and silver-screen slur is captured. From Humphrey Bogart and Groucho Marx to *South Park*'s Eric and Ben Kingsley in *Sexy Beast*, they are packed into this ten-minute gem, venting their spleen and scorn in the most creative ways imaginable. All the greats you remember are here, as well as many that you'll have forgotten. Offensive? Occasionally. Crude? Often. Full of profanities? Oh yes! But I bet you'll be committing some to memory and firing them off yourself next time your ire is stirred.

http://y2u.be/PSEYXWmEse8

THE CUTE ANIMAL ANTIDOTE

Aaaaaaah! Look at the ickle monkey ... What? No! No!

YouTube is full of adorable creatures. Think cute kittens, cheeky chimps, daft dogs and performing parrots. It's enough to make you think the animal world is one big Hallmark birthday card. So what we really need is an animal prepared to push the boundaries of polite behaviour and ham it up for comic effect. It's a tough ask, but the good people of YouTube are always willing to please, so step forward one endearing little monkey with a party trick all of his own...

http://y2u.be/DzZqje04vLE

IS THIS GOING TO BE FOREVER?

The classic *David After Dentist* clip

The answer to eight-year-old David's question really is: yes. His two-minute post-dentist nightmare will be forever viewed as one of YouTube's greatest ever postings. David DeVore Jr had been taken to the dentist to have a tooth removed under anaesthetic. It was David's first surgery and, as his mum couldn't be there, his dad decided to video tape it for her — including his son's philosophical musings on the journey home. David's father first uploaded it to Facebook but, when it hit YouTube, it went mega, reputedly earning the family over $150,000.

http://y2u.be/txqiwrbYGrs

THE REAL LIFE MAJOR TOM

Astronaut sings space classic – in space!

Back in 1969, when David Bowie released the classic single
"Space Oddity", the lyrics seemed a far-off fantasy of an astronaut
singing away in outer space. But in May 2013, just hours before
his planned return to Earth from the International Space Station,
Commander Hadfield cast himself as the song's Major Tom and
picked up his guitar. As the first music video ever shot in space
rocketed up the YouTube charts, picking up a million views in
just 12 hours, the commander was already fielding questions
on whether he might follow it up with Bowie's "Life on Mars".

http://y2u.be/KaOC9danxNo

THE ULTIMATE DEFENCE AGAINST WEAPONS OF MARRIAGE DESTRUCTION

The Better Marriage Blanket – this product will change your life

How could a blanket help you to a better marriage? Does it automatically prevent adultery? Enhance your sex life? Or perhaps create a loving and harmonious relationship? Well, this advert claims the product can do all that by absorbing even the smelliest of farts and preventing what is often known as a Dutch Oven. The blanket, apparently made from the same material the United States military uses to protect against chemical weapons, is the perfect foil to those silent but deadly relationship-wreckers.

http://y2u.be/3yl4nErpGs8

ONE WHEELIE THRILLING RIDE

Crazy stunts from the prince of pedallers

Danny MacAskill can claim to be the first ever street-trials cycling star after this five-minute video went viral in 2009. His film was slick, cut to the soundtrack of cool Band of Horses track "The Funeral", and featured bike stunts most had never witnessed before. The exhilarating film sees Danny tour the streets of Edinburgh, riding along park fences, up trees, down steps and jumping from one building to the next. He soon gave up his job as a bicycle mechanic and is now big-time in Hollywood.

http://y2u.be/Z19zFlPah-o

IS THIS THE RIGHT FLOOR FOR ... AAAAAAAAAAAAAH!

A prank ride in a nightmare lift

Are you ready for the funniest and probably best prank on the whole of YouTube? You better be sure, because this is also the scariest. It's set up by a Brazilian show hosted by top TV presenter Silvio Santos and is brilliantly simple in its execution. All they use is an office lift, a ghoulish-looking small girl holding a doll and some suitable unsuspecting "volunteers". The reaction of the terrified victims is marvellous – watch for the two women adopting the foetal position – but the stunt is so well played out that you'll feel a shiver of fear yourself.

http://y2u.be/8E1YjlHMxAs

THE WRONG GUY

The great BBC News mistaken identity story

Guy Goma, a graduate from the Congo, had turned up at BBC
Television Centre for an interview for a job in data support.
Admittedly, he was a little nervous, but he bravely gave it his
best when the interviewer started asking questions he hadn't
prepped for. Hilariously, Guy had been mistaken for Guy Kewney,
editor of Newswireless.net, who had been summoned to give
his views on the Apple vs Apple court case – live on air. Watch
for yourself as Guy (Goma) handles the situation with some
aplomb. Just 20 minutes later, Goma attended his actual
job interview. He was not hired.

http://y2u.be/zWAvHnfJsOQ

SHAKE A TAIL FEATHER, BABY!

Frostie dances herself viral

YouTube can make a celebrity out of just about anybody – or anything! Take Frostie, a 22-year-old Bare-Eyed Cockatoo, who here makes her YouTube bow, dancing impressively in time to "Shake a Tail Feather". That clip has subsequently been viewed over seven million times and Frostie and her silky moves have been back to the site, shaking her stuff to "Jailhouse Rock", "Whip My Hair", "Hold On I'm Coming" and others. There's even a video of Frostie teaching Avis, a parakeet, a few steps. Dancing-animal aficionados might also want to look up *Hot Salsa Dog* or *Break Dancing Gorilla*.

http://y2u.be/0bt9xBuGWgw

YOUTUBE'S GOT TALENT

25 Things He Hates About Facebook

Julian Smith is a genuine YouTube superstar, who writes, directs and acts in his own mini-masterpieces. In 2009 the then 22-year-old produced this diatribe in response to Facebook's incredibly irritating 25 Random Things About Me survey. His rant went viral and shot him to fame, but Julian was no flash in the pan and a number of other hilarious videos followed. If you like this, try *Racist Coffee*, *Malk* or *Mr Timn in Candyland*. Each one racked up the hits until Julian built more than a million subscribers to his channel and over 250 million views in total.

http://y2u.be/PVA047JAQsk

SIT BACK AND ENJOY!

A brilliant set-up from the prankster master of disguise

YouTube is full of excellent pranks, but it has made the trickster's life seriously tough. It's now a real challenge to come up with a prank idea that no one has seen before, but celebrity magician Rich Ferguson seems to be a master of the art. Search on *Sneeze Head Off* for his previous stunning viral video (you could have a good guess what he does!) but, before that, take a look at this ingenious tomfoolery. In order to shock the pants off people in a coffee shop, Rich disguises himself as … well, you need to see it to believe it!

http://y2u.be/oKGerjB-d1w

HAVING A *JAWS* MOMENT

A Hawaiian fishing trip went crazy – and then viral

The day was going just perfectly for Isaac Brumaghim. He was coasting along in his kayak, enjoying a day's fishing off the coast of Hawaii, and had just begun to reel in a fine-sized tuna. But Isaac wasn't the only one out fishing that day. A huge shark also had its eyes on his catch and was about to steal the fish and scare the living crap out of the fisherman. Now everyone loves a good shark vid, but what really sent this stratospheric was Isaac's absolutely priceless reaction to the creature he later named Chompy the Shark.

http://y2u.be/puNhvXutVjQ

A CONSTANT STRUGGLE FOR SURVIVAL – YADA, YADA, YADA

Time for your close-up Mr Frog

You rarely get to see the real "behind the scenes" footage from those blockbuster wildlife documentaries. Sometimes we hear about how the cameraman spent four months in a tent in the Arctic waiting for a particular fox to walk by or the high-tech microscopic cameras that can film an ant scratching its armpit. But what about the animals? They can spend hours in make-up and rehearsals ("Could we have a little more menace in that roar, please, darling?") and, as we see in this illuminating clip, face a seemingly endless wait to be called for filming…

http://y2u.be/SKRgktzRvZ0

DEER, OH DEER!

The hilarious radio clip that got amplified

YouTube is so full of fantastic videos that it seems a shame to include a radio clip, but how else would you get to hear such a mind-blowing call to a phone-in show as this? After experiencing a number of deer-related accidents while driving, Donna called into her local radio station to complain about how North Dakota's deer-crossing signs are causing animals to get hurt on the highway. As the internet sighed a global "doh!", Donna eventually realized she might have somehow misunderstood the situation, explaining, "In my defence, I grew up in a really small North Dakota town."

http://y2u.be/CI8UPHMzZm8

JACKO GOES STRATOSPHERIC

The original moonwalk – on stage

Michael Jackson is, of course, well represented across YouTube. Any number of his videos are available, but this particular one, in which he sings "Billie Jean" at the Motown 25th anniversary show in 1983, is of historical significance. The performance marks the first ever unveiling of Jacko's signature dance, the moonwalk (3'48" in – just listen to the audience gasp!). Those searching for his inspiration for the dance might care to use YouTube to look up Shalamar singing "Night to Remember" on *Top of the Pops* or the children's TV classic *H.R.Pufnstuf* episode "You Can't Have Your Cake" (2'30" in).

http://y2u.be/pK5EcooSEbk

REACH FOR THE STARS

The original moonwalk — on the moon!

Through YouTube we get instant access to one of the most
famous TV clips ever broadcast. On July 21, 1969 astronaut
Neil Armstrong stepped on to the moon's surface, in the Sea of
Tranquility, declaring, "That's one small step for man, one giant
leap for mankind." It was one of the most amazing moments
ever witnessed on television and can still bring a flutter to
the heart — especially when you think that Apollo 11
made it to the moon using a computer a hundred times
less powerful than your mobile phone!

http://y2u.be/RMINSD7MmT4

CALL OF DUTY – FOR REAL

Helmet camera footage of Taliban firefight

Private Ted Daniels was part of a US Army team on a reconnaissance and intelligence-gathering mission in Afghanistan. When the soldiers encountered a Taliban ambush, the subsequent firefight was recorded on his helmet camera – and later uploaded to YouTube. As the squad found themselves pinned down by machine-gun fire, Private Daniels ventured into the open to draw fire away from them. At this point he turns on the camera and captures two incredible minutes of frightening, adrenaline-pumping real-life warfare. Viewers will be relieved to know that, despite being hit four times, the soldier survived without serious injury.

http://y2u.be/rLHU-_OhT8g

ATTACK OF THE KILLER CARP

A family outing on a small river gets wild

Looking for a fishing trip where you don't spend hours sitting by a river wondering if there are actually any fish down there? You could try Spoon River in Illinois, USA, where the silver carp seem so keen to get caught they jump into the boat. One of those amazing freaks-of-nature videos, this clip shows a family almost under attack from flying fish. The phenomenon is explained by the silver carp being incredibly efficient at reproduction, but also super-skittish, so they literally leap in fear at the approach of a motor boat.

http://y2u.be/InENM6fwlwE

OFF THE LEASH!

Fenton becomes a dog star

Fenton the Labrador became an internet sensation and then a media celebrity when footage of him taken by a 13-year-old hit YouTube in 2012. Fenton was being taken for a walk in Richmond Park in Surrey, England when he decided to have a little fun chasing the park's famous deer. But what really tickled the world's funny bone was the increasing panic in the voice of his owner, an architect named Max, as he hopelessly chased Fenton, while repeatedly screaming the dog's name.

http://y2u.be/3GRSbr0EYYU

GAGGA GAGGA GOO-GOO?

The most compulsive gobbledegook ever

Time for a cute one: meet Sam and Ren McEntee, twins aged just 17 months. They are barely able to stand and are a good few months away from their first real words, yet they are happy to stop for a good old chinwag and appear to understand each other's baby chat. Could it be a psychic-twin thing or are the kids just mimicking their parents? Needless to say, many have attempted to translate their gurgles, but most are pretty unfunny. Go on, have a go: you could still get yourself a hit...

http://y2u.be/lih0Z2IblUQ

EH SEXY LADY!

The song that took over the world

Who would have thought a podgy, ageing rapper, unknown
outside South East Asia, would become the King of YouTube?
In 2012, Park Jae-sang, under his moniker PSY, released a
cheeky dance video to his song "Gangnam Style" and the rest,
as they say, is hysteria. By the start of 2013 the song had topped
music charts in more than 30 countries, its dance moves had
been attempted by everyone from Madonna to David Cameron
to UN Secretary General Ban Ki-moon – who hailed it as a
"force for world peace" – and it was heading for 1.5 billion
views: the highest figure ever recorded.

http://y2u.be/9bZkp7q19f0

HIP HOP HURRAH!

Fun rhyming about two-timing

A novelty rap song. Hmmm, you're probably thinking, that doesn't sound too promising. But hey, this is Emmanuel Hudson, an Atlanta-based rapper who goes by the name Kosher, and he's been going viral with a series of genuinely funny songs about life in the hood and all. "Why You Asking All Them Questions?" teams Hudson with comedian Spoken Reasons in a rap about relationship breakdown – the things she says and the chat he comes back with. It's a clever enough song, but it's the crazy facial expressions that Hudson manages to produce that really pull in the hits.

http://y2u.be/gwUX4cSwrRk

QUICK ON THE DRAW

The self-proclaimed Circle Line Champ

Without YouTube there are so many talents that would remain hidden from the world. Take teacher Alex Overwijk: if it wasn't for the global power of the web he'd still be impressing his small classes with his skill for drawing a near-perfect freehand circle 1m (3ft 3in) in diameter in less than a second and spinning them a yarn about being the "World Freehand Circle Drawing Champion". Thanks to YouTube, however, Alex's proficiency has been viewed over seven million times and now there actually is a World Championship, though Alex hasn't won yet!

http://y2u.be/eAhfZUZiwSE

EVIAN MIX THE BABY FORMULA PERFECTLY

Babies on wheels! What's not to love?

Multi-national corporate businesses with their big-bucks advertising-agency accounts are desperate for an online foothold. Imagine the brainstorming meeting at Evian's ad agency when they discussed their new ad. "Cute babies! Everyone loves 'em!" shouts one. "Can we have an iconic setting – maybe Central Park?" proffers another. "How about some rad stunts?" mumbles the shy, nerdy guy in the corner. But guess what? Somehow it worked. They produced a fantastic ad that has passed 60 million views and has been recognized by the *Guinness Book of Records* as the most viewed online advertisement ever.

http://y2u.be/XQcVllWpwGs

THE MAN WHO FELL TO EARTH

Felix Baumgartner's astonishing sky dive

It was an extraordinary "event", which a record eight million people around the world watched live and open-mouthed on YouTube. On October 14, 2012, Felix Baumgartner leapt out of a helium-filled balloon 39,040m (128,100ft) above the New Mexico desert. It took him 10 minutes to descend to Earth. Just under five of those minutes were spent in freefall and at one point he hurtled towards the ground turning at a rate of 60 revolutions per minute. This 90-second mini-documentary, including wonderful photography from the balloon, perfectly captures the story and the drama of his 1,287km/ph (800mph) world-record-breaking sky dive.

http://y2u.be/FHtvDA0W34I

THERE'S SOMETHING ABOUT MARY

A trailer for a wholly different and totally scary *Mary Poppins*

There are some pretty twisted filmmakers out there in YouTube world. Who in their right mind would take the sweetest children's film ever made and turn it into an 18-rated horror? OK, this is just a trailer, but just imagine what they would do to the whole film! It is, naturally, an incredibly funny work of genius; Julie Andrews is made to look positively demonic and the cute children look petrified. If this tickles you, then maybe you should search for *The Dark Knight Trailer Recut – Toy Story 2* or the *Sleepless in Seattle Recut*.

http://y2u.be/2T5_0AGdFic

NOTHING TO SNEEZE AT

Meet Emerson – superstar in a nappy

The battle for the cutest baby on YouTube is hard fought, but
five-and-a-half-month-old Emerson has to be one of the front
runners. Nearly 50 million views suggest the little chap, who
looks completely terrified when his mum blows her nose, then
immediately laughs hysterically when she stops, has the market
pretty much sewn up, all because his mum figured out how to
upload a video that day and decided to share her son's amusing
moment with friends and family. Emerson, who had no say in the
matter, is probably already dreading telling his school mates…

http://y2u.be/N9oxmRT2YWw

WHEN SCIENCE EXPERIMENTS GO BAD...

Coke and Mentos – an explosive combination

Mixing Coke and Mentos to produce a rocket-type blast is a classic home-science experiment with added suspense provided by the unpredictable nature of the explosion. So, of course, you'll find all manner of videos recording people's adventures with their cornershop products – some more impressive than others. This is a cool one, though, that went viral because of the sheer danger of the exploding projectile. You could also check out some of the more interesting variations, from a C & M-driven rocket car to a gory human-stomach-explosion version.

http://y2u.be/g4kBNBEJKD8

PICK A CARD...

The self-proclaimed "best card trick in the world"

Perhaps not the best, but still pretty impressive – and, with 18 million views, it can certainly claim to be the most viewed card trick on YouTube. The unseen magician asks the internet to pick a card, any card, and deals out some awesome results. It's simple and clearly executed – but there's no explanation of how it's done. Some of the below-the-line comments do attempt to give the trick away but, nevertheless, it is guaranteed to leave you slack-jawed.

http://y2u.be/2KrdBUFeFtY

SAW HIS POST, NOW I'M A BELIEBER

12-year-old Justin Bieber's debut video

In early 2007 Justin Bieber (then 12 years old) performed at a local singing competition. His mother posted the performance on YouTube for family and friends and continued to upload young Justin's performances as his viewers grew from hundreds to thousands. When music executive Scooter Braun discovered Bieber's vids, he was bowled over. Tracking down Justin to his Ontario home, Braun recorded him and introduced him to R&B star Usher. The high-pitched, baby-faced singer's meteoric rise made him the greatest YouTuber ever and his videos continue to be viewed by millions — although they have also garnered a record number of "thumbs-down" dislikes.

http://y2u.be/csymVmm1xTw

JACKSON IN THE JAILHOUSE

Setting the bars high

"No mere mortal can resist the evil of the thriller." So claims Vincent Price at the beginning of Michael Jackson's legendary video. Well, they may not actually be evil, but the 1,500 murderers, dealers and other criminals resident at a high-security prison in the Philippines proved pretty irresistible when their dance routine hit YouTube in 2007. Over 50 million hits later, their success spawned copycat performances, flash mobs and even robot dances, and led to the prisoners taking on other songs and even erecting an audience platform i
n their exercise yard.

http://y2u.be/hMnk7lh9M3o

WOOF! WOOF! ... MIAOW?

Cat caught out in identity crisis

Those pussycats can be pretty clever as well as cute. Whoever would have guessed that the soothing purring and plaintive wailing was all just a front? (Well, apart from the 15 million or so people who have viewed this extraordinary and very funny clip.) What makes it really special is the way the cat seems to be embarrassed to be caught out. Some seem to seek a scientific response to the phenomenon telling us, "Cats don't know they shouldn't bark." Duh! But more agree with the sentiment in the comments that reads, "I come and watch this when I'm having a bad day."

http://y2u.be/aP3gzee1cps

YOUTUBE GETS MESSI

The world's best footballer in glorious, golden, illustrated animation

In 2012 Barcelona and Argentina footballer Lionel Messi was named the FIFA World Player of the Year for the fourth year in a row. To recognize possibly the greatest player the planet has ever seen, Adidas commissioned football artist Richard Swarbrick to make this amazing tribute video. Swarbrick had established his reputation with a similarly styled, stripped-down animation of Tottenham Hotspur's Gareth Bale, but Messi gets the full treatment in a gold-tinged work of art that highlights the footballing genius in all his dribbling, shooting, and even heading glory.

http://y2u.be/ma4AkKgxzxc

MAHNA MAH!

The great Muppets *Bohemian Rhapsody* cover

The first upload on the Muppets Studio Channel was *Meh!*, featuring old Statler and Waldorf discussing the Muppets' move to the internet, but it wasn't until 2010 and the arrival of *Bohemian Rhapsody* – 10 million views in two weeks – that the world realized what its favourite site had been missing. If you're looking for more, try *Ode to Joy*, *Danny Boy* or *Pöpcørn* with the Swedish Chef. Pick from the Studio Channel and you often get Statler and Waldorf's comments at the end. Although just as critical, they knock the spots off the usual below-the-line puerile nonsense!

http://y2u.be/tgbNymZ7vqY

I WANNA HOLD YOUR HAND

The Brad and Angelina of the otter world

Heavens above, aren't the human race a soppy lot? How on earth did we manage to tear ourselves away from gawping at baby animals to ever leave the savannah? This video, shot at the Vancouver Aquarium, has had nearly 20 million people exclaiming, "Awwwww! So sweet!" Before you join them, let's introduce a little scientific knowledge by pointing out that these sea otters, Nyac and Milo, are not holding hands like humans, but engaging in a natural instinct called rafting, which prevents them from floating away from each other in rough waters.

http://y2u.be/epUk3T2Kfno

A SPORTING GLANCE

A costly drop at the baseball

Sporting clips are all over YouTube and it just takes a simple search to find your favourite player, team or whatever, so we're looking for something a little different here. This clip is from a Taiwanese baseball game between the Taipei Brother Elephants and Taoyuan's Lamigo Monkeys, but the action is in the stands as a ball is hit way up into the cheap seats. However, you have to watch it out for the money shot. As the camera lingers on one spectator, we – and he – catch the look on the face of his disappointed, disgusted wife sitting right next to him. Priceless.

http://y2u.be/LX-AzfLkWtY

LIVING THE DREAM

Susan Boyle's momentous first TV appearance

This is one of the most heart-warming videos on YouTube. Despite, or even *because of*, the presence of smug Simon and pompous Piers, the appearance of an unassuming 47-year-old bringing the house down still brings a lump to the throat. Susan Boyle belting out "I Dreamed a Dream" from *Les Misérables* on her 2009 *Britain's Got Talent* audition became the most-watched video of that year. It picked up 66 million views in just one week and launched the career of one of the most unlikely candidates for stardom.

http://y2u.be/RxPZh4AnWyk

QUITE LITERALLY BRILLIANT

Sing what you see

Music videos were once simple affairs – just a straightforward performance of the song. But then they got clever with little stories, vignettes of epic films or, often, hard-to-make-out and confusing nonsense. Literal versions are a genre of videos that set this to rights. It's the same video, but with the words altered to match the pictures and it's surprising just how amusing it can be. Watch this one of A-Ha's "Take on Me" and you'll get the idea. Then maybe try the literal versions of Bonnie Tyler's "Total Eclipse of the Heart" or David Bowie's "China Girl".

http://y2u.be/8HE9OQ4FnkQ

WILFUL DESTRUCTION?
OH YES!

The best product demonstration ever

"Everybody knows that the iPhone can make phone calls, play movies and music, surf the web, and a lot more. But will it blend? That is the question." *Will It Blend?* videos are a series of questions asked by Blendtec founder Tom Dickson as he tests out the power of his line of blenders. Who wouldn't want to watch an iPhone ground into iDust? In his other *Will It Blend?* videos, Tom is found blitzing credit cards, marbles and Big Macs and creating a new dish, cochicken, by blending chicken and Coke. Yummy!

http://y2u.be/qg1ckCkm8YI

READ MY LIPS!

The lip-synching genius of Keenan Cahill

What's really amazing is that this teenager, miming to a chart hit in front of a mirror (OK, webcam) like millions of others since pop music began, has become a global celebrity. To be fair, Keenan Cahill is pretty good at the whole lip-synch act. His performances are understated but very comicall. This video, Katy Perry's "Teenage Dream", led to his big break when Katy herself saw it and tweeted "I heart you" to Keenan. He never looked back, subsequently appearing with Katy, the *Glee* cast, 50 Cent and others.

http://y2u.be/lm_n3hg-Gbg

WHAT'S YOUR MEME?

Hold your breath, it's the *Underwater Harlem Shake*…

The *Harlem Shake* meme could have been what YouTube was invented for: it lasts just 30 seconds, is simple to shoot and edit and requires little dancing talent. The form developed from a 1980s dance track, through a dull dance by Filthy Frank to a group of Australian teenagers who call themselves the Sunny Coast Skate. From there it went whoosh and within a month everyone from Norwegian Army platoons to underground miners (later sacked for breaching safety restrictions) were pointedly ignoring a single dancer for 15 seconds before suddenly finding themselves in costume and going crazy. A meme is that simple!

http://y2u.be/QkNrSpqUr-E

SCAREDY CAT

Awww! Is the poor little kitty shwocked?

Feline videos proliferate in such abundance that we could almost rename it MewTube, but this one is at least funny as well as endearing. It's even been called the cutest video in the world. This kitten is called Atilla Fluff (at this point, you need to do that "putting your fingers down your throat" mime), she's a couple of months old and her talent is … she does a great impression of being one surprised little moggy. More cynical viewers might prefer the humour of the *Somewhat Surprised Kitty* parody video, though.

http://y2u.be/0Bmhjf0rKe8

FRUITY ENTERTAINMENT

Hey! Hey! It's annoying orange

There's this orange, right? It's got a mouth and eyes and everything (well, no arms and legs, obviously) and it lives on the kitchen table, spending its time calling out, insulting, making bad jokes and generally irritating the other fruit and vegetables. Stop. Don't flick past just yet. As irritating and childish as it seems, there's something very funny going on here and 30 million hits and a whole channel of vids don't lie. Go on, give it a go. You might find a little immaturity in a citrus fruit makes you smile.

http://y2u.be/ZN5PoW7_kdA

POTTERING ABOUT

Potter Puppet Pals prove popular

In 2006 J.K. Rowling's Harry Potter books and the film adaptations were a global success, but HP still had one more realm to conquer – the internet. Filmmaker Neil Cicierega left behind his avant-garde animations to produce simple Potter puppet plays. Well, almost. Harry, Ron, Hermione and the others were there, but they were different, and funny – as if Neil had never even read the books. It was this episode, *The Mysterious Ticking Noise*, which sent the Potter Puppet Pals series hyper, and seven years later it is still ranked as YouTube's 22nd most-viewed video.

http://y2u.be/Tx1XIm6q4r4

IF YOU LIKE IT, YOU CAN PUT A TUNE TO IT

Just how much does Debbie love cats (in song)?

Thanks to modern technology — more specifically an app called Songify — you can turn literally anything anyone ever says into a song. The Gregory Brothers have proved themselves the YouTube masters of remixes and songifications (if that's even a word). Their biggest hits are (a slightly dubious) *The Bed Intruder Song* and *Winning — a Song by Charlie Sheen*, but here they put their magic to a video that was already YouTube gold in which Debbie gets a little over emotional about her love of cats.

http://y2u.be/sP4NMoJcFd4

A TRUE CULINARY SENSATION

The song with the buttery biscuit base

Masterchef has been one of the most popular shows on our TV screens for years now, but Masterchef synesthesia took the United Kingdom's staid presenters Gregg Wallace and John Torode and turned them into some kind of dancehall sensation. Swede Mason is a true alchemist; his mash-up turns a minute's recorded foody jibberish into ambrosia. It has everything a perfect hit needs — a catchy repeated phrase, a great beat, a trippy vibe and two nodding middle-aged blokes. Bet you can't help joining in on the "wobble, wobble, wobble" bit.

http://y2u.be/IfeyUGZt8nk

HIGH NOON AT THE WATER HOLE

It's Buffalos versus Lions in the African Safari Cup

One of YouTube's most watched nature clips, this video
was filmed by an amateur filmmaker in September 2004 at
a watering hole in Kruger National Park, South Africa. As an
almighty scrap breaks out between a pride of lions and a herd of
buffalo – with an intervention by a hungry crocodile – we hear
the squeals and excitement of the safari-goers, who are hardly
able to keep their khaki shorts dry at the sight of exotic animals
attempting to rip each other apart. Whose side are you on?

http://y2u.be/LU8DDYz68kM

DANCING WITH THE STJARS

Football's goal celebration kings

Iceland might not be the obvious home of classic football videos, but, via YouTube, Stjarnan FC have carved out a reputation as the ruling champions – of goal celebrations. The team sit proudly in the top tier of Icelandic football, but it's these amusing cameo performances that attract the fans. Not for them the shirt-off antics or soppy hand hearts of our Premier League heroes. Stjarnan's "dances" vary from landing a fish to throwing a grenade and from ballroom dancing to riding a human bicycle. Indeed, you feel they might spend more time choreographing their moves than actually training.

http://y2u.be/Z0GByFJ-zMQ

LET ME GIVE YOU MY CARD

Introducing the ancient art of business card throwing

Although beloved in the 1980s, business cards aren't much use for anything in these high-tec days, except maybe entering competitions in restaurants, but this guy has found a use for his – as a super-sharp, super-accurate, martial-arts-type missile. If this impressive demonstration inspires you to take up a sport that is increasingly popular (it says here), all you need is a good supply of business cards, good hand-eye co-ordination, a strong and supple wrist – and a complete lack of anything useful to do with your time.

http://y2u.be/FVq0HdiM-Ok

BARK SEAT DRIVER

Meet Porter, the world's first driving dog

Now we've seen so many clips of cats looking cute, making human-type noises and, well, looking even more cute – but they can't touch their canine cousins. Dogs can lead the blind, fetch your slippers and now – those pussies are going to have to go some to beat this – there's a dog that can drive! Who knows where this will end? Traffic jams on the way to the park? Doggie chauffeurs? A Chum-sponsored F1 team? But one thing is for sure – you're going to be spending a whole lot more on car-upholstery cleaning.

http://y2u.be/BWAKOJ8Uhzk

"DADDY'S HOME!"

Horror recut as wholesome family entertainment

In this trailer for a nice romantic comedy, an author suffering from writer's block takes his family to an empty hotel, where he bonds with his lonely young son and reignites his love for his wife. It's even got a bright, happy title: *Shining*. As you may have guessed by now, this video does the exact opposite of *Scary Mary Poppins* (see page 86) to Jack Nicholson's movie *The Shining*. Don't be taken in, though, folks. *The Shining* is not actually a feel-good movie. It is, of course, a well-known musical...

http://y2u.be/KmkVWuP_sO0

OUCH! SH**! OMG!

Knock yourself out with an "Epic Fail" compilation

"Epic Fail" is YouTubese for something going wrong. Type the words into the search box and you'll be rewarded with any number of videos full of people falling over, crashing into things, sitting on collapsing objects, being spat at by zoo animals – the kind of thing TV compilation shows love. This links to the most popular of these, which has over 50 million views – that's a whole lot of people enjoying watching other folk getting hurt or humiliated. What a sad critique of society. Still, that one where he falls off the bike is *so* funny...

http://y2u.be/Ujwod-vqyqA

SINGALONGALLAMA

The catchiest ditty on YouTube

Now what have we here? Something for the young at heart.
"Here's a llama, there's a llama, and another little
llama, fuzzy llama, funny llama – llama llama duck –
llama llama, cheesecake llama, tablet, brick, potato llama,
llama llama, mushroom llama – llama llama duck..."
Don't knock it: the video has more than 40,000 likes and
has spawned Barack Obama, Yoda and Harry Potter
versions. Now don't pretend you won't be going
back and learning the words.

http://y2u.be/HbPDKHXWILQ

SILENT WITNESS

The assassination of JFK

YouTube also serves as a source for some priceless historical footage. This clip, filmed in 1963, was not even broadcast on television until 1975. Now we have free access to the most famous 36-second film of the 20th century. Clothing-company boss Abraham Zapruder took his 8mm cine camera to the Dealey Plaza to record John F. Kennedy's motorcade as it passed through Dallas. By chance, he chose one of the best vantage points possible to record the assassination of the President. Still shocking and graphic, the footage was instrumental in both supporting and disproving the conspiracy theory of a second assassin on the grassy knoll.

http://y2u.be/kMBCfxIqP-s

MATT GETS SHIRTY

A pointless but very entertaining world record

Those YouTubers love a challenge, and when Matt McAllister posted his successful attempt to set the Guinness World Record for the most T-shirts worn at one time, he certainly started something. The Phoenix-based radio host had put on over 100lb in four hours by the time he slipped on his 155th T-shirt in sizes ranging from small through to 10XL, but he'd got his name in the famous book. His record was short-lived though, with many others taking him on. The latest record stands at 247 and is there on YouTube, but Matt's attempt remains the original and by far the best fun.

http://y2u.be/r6tlw-oPDBM

STREETS OF SAN FRANCISCO

A high-octane stunt ride in the heart of the city

It's a tyre-shredding, donut-pulling, jump-drift-driving feast on the streets of San Francisco as rally driver Ken Block takes his Ford Fiesta (not like yours, no) around the city like he's running very late for an important appointment. This is top stunt driving with Ken taking sharp curves at 160km/ph (100mph), spinning round cable cars and going airborne over San Francisco's famous city hills. Fortunately, the city seems eerily desolate, so Ken doesn't have to worry about encountering any grannies on zebra crossings or getting stuck behind an ice-cream van.

http://y2u.be/LuDN2bClyus

MURDER BY DEATH

The Top 10 hilarious movie murders

You'll find Top 10s of just about everything, but this one is quite special. Have you got a favourite movie death? Well, it's probably not in this list. They are not all obscure B-movie fatalities, but they are all gross, violent or just very, very funny. Who couldn't love the self-combusting-out-of-pure-anger bodyguard or not find the murder by frisbee strangely compelling? The only criticism? Check out the extraordinary *Worst Movie Death Scene Ever* clip. Surely that should be on this list, too?

http://y2u.be/be7nHzijyGE

GRIN AND BEAR IT

Man versus bear in one of the best commercials ever

The John West Salmon Bear Fight has been named the funniest advert of all time. Yes, you may have seen it already, but it's always worth another viewing. The ad begins as a nature documentary about bears fishing for salmon. Then a screaming fisherman suddenly runs into the scene, determined to fight the bears for the best fish. Despite the bears' natural fighting ability and dazzling kung fu moves, the fisherman has a couple of dirty tricks up his sleeve.

http://y2u.be/CVS1UfCfxIU

BEST BY A LONG CHALK

The amazing 3D pavement artist

There are some things you wouldn't believe if you didn't see them taking shape before your eyes. If the most you ever learned in art was how to make trees look like they're far away by drawing them very small, you'll be amazed by the talent of artist Chris Carlson. With just a set square, a ruler and some chalk, he draws a brilliant three-dimensional Super Mario vaulting over a game controller — on the pavement! The 11 hours of intense labour are reduced to four mesmerizing, time-lapsed minutes as his masterpiece takes shape.

http://y2u.be/U2juYr2Xjeo

BACK TO THE DRAWING BOARD

The King of YouTube draws his life

Ryan Higa is pretty much the biggest YouTube celebrity around. He has nearly eight million subscribers to the short comedy films and sketches on his channel. So when Ryan joined the Draw My Life fad that was sweeping YouTube, folk sat up and took notice. The meme involves YouTubers' autobiographies accompanied by their drawings of stick men. Yes, OK, but Ryan is a consummate artist and his story, from birth to present, is brilliantly told, wonderfully drawn and totally, totally inspiring.

http://y2u.be/KPmoDYayoLE

LABOUR OF LOVE

A portrait of a pregnancy

Time-lapse portraits are often an interesting way to waste your time on YouTube. The fascinating *She Takes a Photo Every Day*, which covers five years in just a minute, is one such project. This time-lapse story of a pregnancy condensing nine months into 90 seconds is even better. Taking a picture in the same pose throughout, it documents the growth of the expectant mother's bump and the subtle ways in which life changes around her. It's incredibly sweet, has a nice sense of humour and has a great and creative ending – in every sense of the word.

http://y2u.be/nKnfjdEPlJ0

JUST KIDDING!

The cruellest prank ever?

There are some things in life you just can't do. Like giving the opposition a penalty at Old Trafford, telling Eamonn Holmes he's carrying an extra pound or two or asking Prince Charles if he'll ever be king. Telling your kids you've eaten their hard-earned Halloween sweets is in the same league – so expect the worst to happen. US chat-show host Jimmy Kimmell asked his viewers to do just that and film the little treasures' reactions. The result? A fabulous montage of spoiled brats, sugar-addicted toddlers and a couple of sweethearts that make you instantly forgive all the rest!

http://y2u.be/WOlpdd7y8MI

A WORLD AT HIS FINGERTIPS

A beautifully woven holographic love story

Imagine you could create a city for the one you love, with streets, houses and buildings loaded with meaning. What would it look like? Paris? Venice? Harlow New Town? World Builder, a captivating ten-minute story by Hollywood special-effects man Bruce Banit, explores just such an idea. It starts with a guy in an empty space and follows him as he constructs a perfect world around him using holographic tools. It's engrossing, hauntingly beautiful and emotionally charged. By the closing credits you might even be shedding a tear.

http://y2u.be/VzFpg271sm8

IT'S A BEAUTIFUL WORLD

Films that make our world look like toytown

If you're told that Keith Loutit, the genius behind this three-minute jewel of a film, uses tilt-shift photography to achieve his unique filmed style, would you be any the wiser? Enough to say that the fabulous real but miniature world he creates is bewitching. Colours are brilliant, movement is jerky and everyone and everything looks like it is in some kind of wonderland. Bathtub (this is Bathtub IV) is actually Sydney and, in his other films, Keith shows he can also give London, Singapore and other destinations a similarly enchanting veneer.

http://y2u.be/LkrtYRxGyuo

CAN YOU KICK IT?

When breakdancing goes bad

Streetdance and breakdancing are popular YouTube genres and so are cute little toddlers, so just imagine what a viral hit you get if you combine them. Of course, you could search for "Tiny kid break dancing" and watch six-year-old Jaylen bustin' his moves on American TV, but this is much, much more fun. This ad-hoc Times Square show is smooth and well-rehearsed. Now just watch this kid go. He throws some tricky moves... That could be a helicopter, that's maybe something like a double pencil drop followed by a suicide corkscrew and here comes the best bit... They call it the streetfighter!

http://y2u.be/NqS9N7WJOFY

AMAZING BOUNCING BEAR

A tranquilizer dart, a trampoline and a falling bear...

Some American towns have a real problem with hungry bears encroaching into urban areas. They leave their rubbish everywhere, take up valuable room on public transport and deliver quite a shock when leaping out of trees. So, as this video illustrates, US authorities are empowered to humiliate them and send the disgraced creatures back home to tell their pals of their unfortunate experiences in the big city. We're waiting for the video of the one made to perform on *America's Got Talent* but, in the meantime, we can make do with this shameful exercise.

http://y2u.be/Pa1pIO4_IUY

THE GUILTY PARTY BOY

Australian teenager who became an internet hero

Corey Worthington – what a guy! Millions of teenagers around the world tipped a baseball cap to the 16-year-old Aussie who put on a party to end all parties – and refused to grovel in apology. With his parents on holiday, Corey threw a party, advertised it on social networks and seemed delighted that a few hundred turned up, trashed the place and his neighbours' cars, and fought with police. Watch Corey make mincemeat of the haughty news presenter – and never, but never, ask him to take off his shades!

http://y2u.be/xc0CB6URrV0

IT'S A SHEEP SHOT, BUT IT WORKS!

A viral victory for sheep choreography

As tantalizing as the title *Extreme Sheep LED Art* is, what this Samsung-sponsored video delivers is altogether more gobsmacking. It's a version of *One Man and His Dog* if said man wasn't a Welsh farmer in a flat cap but a groovy artist type with a crazy haircut. Putting a flock of sheep in light-studded jackets and herding them into well-rehearsed shapes around the Brecon Beacons produces the most incredible results. Not to give anything away, but it's not often you come away from a farm thinking the Pong was fantastic...

http://y2u.be/D2FX9rviEhw

LET'S TWIST AGAIN

Team Hot Wheels pulls off a record-breaking stunt

Remember Hot Wheels, the kids' toy cars that performed stunts on bright-orange tracks? Well, they have produced real-life daredevil vids as full-scale versions of their cars (on orange tracks!) break all kinds of stunt records. Elsewhere you can find double loops and the longest jump in a four-wheeled vehicle, but this corkscrew jump, first performed in the James Bond movie *The Man with the Golden Gun*, is the most fun. Hollywood stuntman Brent Fletcher uses a split-level ramp to spin his souped-up buggy through the air at a rate of 230 degrees per second for 28m (92ft).

http://y2u.be/s48hfG0bi_I

KITTENS, FIREMEN, TEQUILA

Could a kitten-saving fireman save your evening?

Make It with a Fireman – this must be one for the ladies and this
tequila company goes straight for a knock-out blow. "What do
women like?" they've asked themselves. "Why, men in uniform,
kittens, a sense of humour and a strong margarita," they've
answered. "Being a fireman is more than putting out blazes
and giving kittens CPR," says the hunky, stripped-to-the-waist
fireman. "Sometimes my duty demands I fan the flames."
Patronizing, a little sexist and ridiculously old-fashioned
it may be, but it's very funny and it's pulling in
the views. Maybe it's that cute kitten?

http://y2u.be/cwWnIhFd8gA

THE ICE-DUDE COMETH

German attempts cannonball into frozen pool

Should there ever be a YouTube dictionary, this would have to be the illustration for the entry on *Schadenfreude* (taking pleasure from the misfortunes of others), especially as it, too, is of German origin. Although just a short video of a man jumping into a pool, this really is the perfect clip. It is concise, hilarious and looks horribly painful (without being gory or tragic). You may lack sympathy for our freezing hero in swimming briefs as he indulges in some full-blown machismo and totally arrogant posturing, but the almost inevitable slapstick, his reaction and the contagious hysterics bestow instant forgiveness.

http://y2u.be/VBXKoZQwvDE

THE MOST FAMOUS SNEEZE ON THE PLANET

A panda and her cub go viral

How many views does a clip need before it becomes a YouTube cliché? This one has had over 150 million and must be the most watched 17 seconds on the site. Mao Mao and her cub have been parodied everywhere, had a mention on *South Park* and have even inspired a video game. If you haven't seen it, watch it now – it's worth 17 seconds of your time, promise. If you have seen it, watch it again. Some people have been known to sit all day (usually at work) watching it over and over.

http://y2u.be/FzRH3iTQPrk

INTO THE LION'S DEN

The incredible story of Christian the Lion

In 1969 John Rendall and Ace Berg saw a lion cub for sale in Harrods. They named him Christian and took him back to their London flat. Within a year, Christian had grown to an unmanageable size and they were forced to arrange his re-introduction to the wild in Africa. Another year passed and his former owners headed out to Kenya to find him. By then, Christian had a new life and his own pride and, so they were told, would never remember them. This video shows just what happened — and remains one of the most heart-warming videos on YouTube.

http://y2u.be/btuxO-C2IzE

GUIDE TO BATHROOM ETTI-CAT!

He's a cat flushing the toilet

Let's face it. You could upload a 50-second clip of a cat doing virtually anything and earn thousands of YouTube hits in days. So, credit to dragonzice1 for bothering to edit together a series of cats who are clever enough to have mastered pulling the flush in the toilet (a feat many human men have still to master on a regular basis). Even better, there's a rather catchy ditty to accompany the footage of these masterful moggies… Altogether now, "He's a cat – miaow – flushing the toilet – he's a cat…"

http://y2u.be/saQcnblLinc

CAN YOU FEEL THE FORCE?

A mini Darth Vader in the best advert ever

The most shared ad of all time, this was Volkswagen's effort for America's 2011 Superbowl break, the Valhalla of TV advertising. "Leaked" on to YouTube a week previously, the commercial had already notched ten million views by the time it was broadcast. It took just a little bit of *Star Wars*, a healthy dollop of cute kid and a shiny new car to make a 60-second advertising legend. The tale was, however, made more poignant when it was revealed that the ad's seven-year-old star, Max Page, had a congenital heart defect and was facing open-heart surgery.

http://y2u.be/1n6hf3adNqk

THE ULTIMATE NUMBERS GAME

Countdown's most awesome moment

This clip has been taken from the golden era of the British daytime word-and-numbers TV game show when it was still hosted by the ever-genial late Richard Whitely and his boffin bombshell assistant Carol Vorderman. The numbers game is a popular part of the show as contestants are given 30 seconds to reach a randomly chosen target total from six pre-selected numbers. Such was Carol's mental maths genius that she could nearly always match the contestants. Then this episode came along… Too clever-clever for you? OK, Philistines, you can search on *Countdown* blooper for clips of rude words making an inadvertent appearance!

http://y2u.be/pfa3MHLLSWI

ROLLING IN THE AISLE

That famous Royal Wedding spoof

In April 2011, as Royal fever hit Britain in anticipation of the wedding of Prince William and Kate Middleton, T-Mobile grasped the opportunity to make a splash with their own version of the wedding entrance. Obviously fearing an "off with their heads" reaction, T-Mobile hung on the right side of tasteful, as various royal lookalikes and a fake archbishop bumped and ground their way down the aisle to an East 17 track. The ad was a viral sensation. Justin Bieber tweeted his enthusiasm to his nine million followers and Prince Harry apparently liked it so much he posted it on his personal Facebook page.

http://y2u.be/Kav0FEhtLug

A MOUSE-EYE VIEW

Incredible hyper-slow-motion footage of a swooping owl

There are some things that bear endless re-viewing in slow-motion: the Zapruder JFK footage, Geoff Hurst's 1966 over-the-line goal or *that* Sharon Stone clip. This superb piece of wildlife footage can certainly join the list. It's an astonishing video in slow motion of a Eurasian Eagle Owl swooping to almost attack the camera lens. Filmed at a thousand frames a second, it reveals just how the bird moves its wings and controls its landing, giving a clear rendering of every individual feather as the owl positions itself to land.

http://y2u.be/SAz1L8DlvBM

HAVING A WHALE OF A TIME

See and believe – the whale they blew up!

Who would have thought that a 40-year-old grainy news story
of a beached whale would attract over three million views? The
story centres around a dead whale lying on the Oregon coastline
back in 1970. When the locals got over the novelty, they started
to notice the smell and demanded something be done.
Fifty-odd sticks of dynamite later, we see the majestic mammal
detonated and, as the reporter says, "The blast blasted blubber
beyond all believable bounds." There are now T-shirts,
a song, a website and, you never know, maybe a West End
musical, commemorating the event.

http://y2u.be/1_t44siFyb4

WELCOME TO HAMSTER-JAM

The rise and rise of the gangsta hamsters

What's the best way to advertise a trendy compact car aimed at young women? If you said hip-hop hamsters, go straight to your nearest ad agency and demand yourself a job. The gold-chained, headphone-wearing, hoodied-up dancing hamsters have driven right over the opposition in ads that saw them eschew the traditional stationary wheel for a set of cool Kia Soul wheels. With over 20 million views, this is the most successful in the series but, if you like the shuffling, rapping rodents, there's minutes more entertainment just waiting for you.

http://y2u.be/4zJWA3Vo6TU

RUMBLE IN THE OUTBACK

Who'd win a fight between an emu and a kangaroo?

This farmyard tussle actually pits two of Australia's favourite creatures against each other. Well, you know what those emus are like after a few too many acacia leaves on a Friday night. And, a little like the scene outside your local kebab house of a weekend, there's a lot of posturing and posing, but not a lot in the way of knockout blows. If you listen carefully, you can even catch one of the emus screaming, "Leave him, Shane, he's not worth it!"

http://y2u.be/d9OBqYbZ99c

LOSING IT BIG TIME

The strange story of the angry German kid

We've all been frustrated by video games. You're on the verge of reaching the next level and bang goes your last life or they put a ridiculous challenge in that you are never going to solve in a million years — but this lad has gone ballistic and the game hasn't even started yet. OK, watch it now before you read the next bit. In 2006 the post went viral, spawning numerous parodies and tributes, but a few years later it emerged that the whole thing was staged. Do you believe that confession? Many remain convinced this is the real "losing it" deal.

http://y2u.be/q8SWMAQYQf0

YES SIR, I CAN BOOGIE

From Elvis to Jay-Z in seven minutes

It took a thirtysomething, bald white guy to nail the ultimate YouTube dance video. Judson Laipply's witty, energetic and imaginative sketch called *The Evolution of Dance* was, at one time, YouTube's most watched and top-rated video. Judson twists, body pops, robots, breakdances and headbangs his way through over 30 songs in a six-minute routine that has racked up over 200 million views. It's entertaining enough, but you might feel it's better performed by a real robot! In which case, check out *Evolution of Dance* by NAO Robot and see for yourself.

http://y2u.be/dMH0bHeiRNg

DOGGY STYLE

An exercise video with a difference – a big difference

There's some really odd stuff on YouTube. Yes, really. It's not uncommon to stumble across somewhat strange, nay bizarre, videos, but this one is just right out there, way past weird – and it's somehow important to share it. It's called *Poodle Exercise with Humans*. We are told that it's a word-for-word parody of a workout video by US celebrity Susan Powter and was made by Japanese pop artist Nagi Noda. However, there's nothing to warn us that it's completely bonkers, totally mesmerizing and could well lead to some disturbing, not to say surreal, nightmares.

http://y2u.be/g8hsl6Y2L-U

"WHAT? YOU ATE ALL THE MEAT IN THE FRIDGE!"

The ultimate dog tease

"What's up, Rover?"
"It's all cat, cat, cat, isn't it? Haven't they got anything for dogs on YouTube?"
"Well, what about this? It stars a gullible German shepherd dog named Clarke."
"That's great. Click it!"
"It was the big hit in 2011. And Clarke talks – just like you!"
"Yes! That code now, please!"
"You sure? It's all about how his owner ate all the meat in the fridge."
"What!!!"

http://y2u.be/nGeKSiCQkPw

DROP AND ROLL

Rally driver in dramatic cliff-side plunge

This one's for the crash voyeurs, but it's OK — amazingly no one gets hurt. This is from the Race to the Clouds, the annual race that climbs 1,542m (5,000ft) to the summit of Pikes Peak in Colorado. Some vehicles don't make it that far and that was the fate of rally driver Jeremy Foley and his co-driver as they lost control on a bend, rolling over 14 times as they plunged 30m (100ft) down a 45-degree slope into a rock field. For a shorter but just as impressive in-car view of the incident, look at *Jeremy Foley Pikes Peak Crash in Car Video #1*. Rallytastic!

http://y2u.be/JDVLoO8vTXY

TAKING A DIVE

Going for the sympathy vote

This is a great clip because it gets to the root of human behaviour. ATTENTION – I WANT ATTENTION AND I WANT IT NOW! Some of us continue to audition for TV talent shows, but most learn to hold it in. Now, this little fella is determined to get some TLC and is going about it in the only way he knows – crying for sympathy. And if that doesn't work, he's going to try Plan B, which is, er ... more crying for sympathy. The only trouble is, he's been to the Cristiano Ronaldo School of Soccer Diving – and he's kidding no one.

http://y2u.be/_XObo46us_A

MONKEY BUSINESS

This classic animal advert is top banana

Back in the days before YouTube, animals who could talk like humans – and this will amaze many of you – were actually very rare, and most people could get their fix only via the adverts that interrupted the evening's viewing on their newly purchased colour TV sets. If the internet had existed in 1971, this clip would have gone super-viral. It shows that you can still find the old gems online – and stands up to the best that YouTube can offer.

http://y2u.be/HgzEBLa3PPk

IN THE DOGHOUSE

Someone's helped themselves to the Kitty Cat treats...

This is quite possibly the best whodunit on the web. We have incontrovertible evidence found at the crime scene, two suspects and a detective determined to get to the bottom of the matter. But who will crack first? Is there a tell-tale sign that reveals the perpetrator of the heinous crime? Will the guilty party give themselves away? And when the verdict is delivered, will they accept their punishment without complaint? The famous Denver the Guilty Dog is worth every one of its 25 million views!

http://y2u.be/B8ISzf2pryl

A WHOLE NEW BALL GAME

The magical art of contact juggling

Contact juggling: it's a kind of cross between a magic trick, the boring juggling you see on variety shows and a martial art — and it's pretty cool. This clip, in which a small crystal ball appears to be floating in mid air with the "juggler" merely caressing and rolling the ball in order to manipulate it, is a fabulous example of the supposedly ancient art. The mystical-looking sphere is called a fushigi ball, but the magic is all in the hands. Check out the *Fushigi Ball Explained* clip if you want to see how it's done.

http://y2u.be/mbMDI-JSb30

OK, BUT WHERE'S MY BURRITOS?

Mexican music meets Arctic whale in Connecticut

One can't help thinking that surreal artist Salvador Dalí would have absolutely loved YouTube — unfortunately, he died in 1989, a full 16 years before the first post. Where else, apart from Dalí and his friends' work, would you find a mariachi band serenading a Beluga whale? It's not as if Juno from the Marine Life Aquarium in Connecticut can actually hear through the glass and the water, although, to be fair, she does seem to be enjoying and nodding along to the performance — and at least she didn't have to put any money in the hat to get them to move along.

http://y2u.be/ZS_6-IwMPjM

THE HERO HOG

Pig saves baby goat – or does it?

It was earth-shattering. Like the day you found out that Father Christmas wasn't real. This video, which was uploaded to YouTube in September 2012, went viral in hours. It was like a message from above. Everything on Earth is just fine. If a pig can rescue a baby goat, then one day surely we can all live in harmony? Just five months later, the sickening truth was out: the whole thing was staged. It was revealed to have taken a 20-person crew, including animal trainers and scuba divers, to arrange the "stunt". And they wonder why we are all such cynics!

http://y2u.be/g7WjrvG1GMk

GOING NOWHERE – SLOWLY

A classic drunken escalator fail

Real life throws up stuff that is so much funnier than any comedy show. This two-minute clip of late-night life in a London Underground station is simply hilarious. It stars one very drunk Japanese businessman attempting to walk down an up escalator and a kind young woman who desperately tries to point him in the right direction. There's something about the man's steadfast plodding despite his lack of progress and the woman's frustrated but determined refusal to let him keep going all night that brings a smile to your face and a warmth to your cockles.

http://y2u.be/txNmh8i3AyA

DANGEROUS CYCLE-PATH

The New York bike lane vigilante

When the New York police gave Casey Neistat a ticket, fining him for not riding his bike in the cycle lane, they picked on the wrong guy. Casey was already a YouTube star, having produced an iPod-battery warning campaign and other popular movies. So, taking the fine to heart, Casey decides to try sticking to the bike lane as instructed and filming the result. He's making a serious point about the obstacles in his way, but it makes for amusing if painful viewing. If you like this, try Casey's equally witty *Make It Count*.

http://y2u.be/bzE-IMaegzQ

LEAVE CHRIS ALONE.

A heartfelt defence of Britney Spears

Nobody likes a bully, but too few of us are prepared to stand up to them. Chris Crocker is different. In 2008 he uploaded a video of himself speaking in defence of someone he knew named Britney. Apparently, all kinds of bad things were being said about this young woman and Chris was not prepared to put up with it any more. Well, years later we don't know whether the inexcusably hurtful things hurled at Britney have stopped, but we do now know that some pretty terrible things have been said about Chris himself. Enjoy the tear-interrupted, over-hysterical, ridiculously camp rant— but please, leave Chris alone!

http://y2u.be/WqSTXuJeTks

DOG TREAT

***Bizzle Gets Some Dunkers* – great title, great video**

Who has had more YouTube views: the cute, mischievous cat or the faithful, lovable dog? The cat-vs-dog battle is hard fought, so the success of this video led to an appeal from the cat lovers. How can it count as a dog video when the American bulldog clearly has human arms and hands? What kind of monstrous creature is this anyway? From these few minutes, it appears pretty benign and content to sit at the dinner table and munch its way through a snack. Another five million to the canines, though? You decide.

http://y2u.be/bgoDkwwpFx0

TECHNOLOGICAL GENIUS

Brief but brilliant YouTube gag

Afraid of Technology is the best short on YouTube. A video version
of a one-liner, it's a perfectly set-up gag that's over and done
with in five seconds (which is not to say you won't be repeating
it over and over again). There is a definite art to framing the joke
in such a short time, so for some more examples, have a look at:
Drunk Old Man Stopped and Breath Tested by Police,
Pretty Much Everywhere It's Gonna be Hot and the
inspired *Hercules – DISAPPOINTED*.

http://y2u.be/Fc1P-AEaEp8

THINKING INSIDE THE BOX

Meet the World Wide Web's most famous cat

This video features Maru, a Scottish Fold cat who lives in Japan. Now Maru likes boxes – big boxes, small boxes, slim boxes, tiny boxes. Indeed, he loves boxes and that, along with his general cat-ness, is Maru's talent. However, as was nearly once said, there's something about Maru, and his 300-film YouTube channel has over 300,000 subscribers and his videos have been viewed more than 100 million times. Even if you don't like cats, watch this one through because it has a nice, funny ending.

http://y2u.be/2XID_W4neJo

SOMETHING THE CAT BROUGHT IN

Introducing Nora the piano cat

We've kept the cat quota as low as possible, but there's really no avoiding this. As amazing videos go, *Nora: Practice Makes Purr-fect* is right up there (better than *Keyboard Cat* anyhow). Agreed, any old mog can plink plonk along the piano and get some sound out of it, but this cat does truly seem to have some musical talent. The clip features her hard at work composing and playing a duet with (presumably) a human partner. Of course, Mozart was writing a concerto at the age of five, but then he couldn't bring up furballs and lick his own...

http://y2u.be/5fGQLHKx-Y0

EVERYBODY FREEZE!

The great Grand Central freeze

The Freeze is a well-tried flash-mob performance, but it took New York's Improv Everywhere (mentioned elsewhere in these pages) to really pull it off in style. This one involved over 200 "IE Agents" gathering in the main concourse of New York City's iconic Grand Central Station. As travellers bustled through the busy railway station, the agents mingled among them. Suddenly, at the agreed time, they froze in their pose. They then held still for five minutes, while stunned commuters and tourists either joined in or stood wondering just what the hell was going on.

http://y2u.be/jwMj3PJDxuo

SPINE CHILLER

The ultimate dare

We'd say don't try this at home, but, honestly, who would be so stupid? The Children of Poseidon are three blokes from Perth who make some of the most eye-watering videos on YouTube. Having tried setting each other on fire, launching themselves from shopping trollies, eating cat food and supergluing their lips shut, they were still searching for that elusive internet hit. Then they came up with *Cactus Bodyslam*, in which Jeffabel Poseidon hurls himself semi-naked at a large spiny cactus plant. It is painful to watch, agonizing for the Aussie idiot, but it did the trick.

http://y2u.be/PHSJCMkUa9Y

PISTOL PARENTING

Teenager's dad dishes out some tough love

If you want to cause an internet rumpus, try taking on the teenage psyche. An American parent called Tommy Jordan became exasperated with his 15-year-old daughter Hannah after she had posted a letter on her Facebook profile, criticizing him and her mother. His response was unusual, to say the least. He recorded his own, alarming but hilarious, message and posted it on her Facebook wall. When that was uploaded to YouTube, the whole teenage world had a hissy fit on Hannah's behalf, while parents stood shoulder-to-shoulder with their new hero. Are you ready to join the fracas?

http://y2u.be/kl1ujzRidmU

FRUIT SHOOT

Bringing a phone game to life

Fruit Ninja is one of the most popular smartphone games ever. It's a simple affair in which you slash fruit in half with a samurai sword, but it has proved as addictive as sugar. So what better wheeze than to play the game for real? Out in the woods someone throws some fruit at a guy in fancy dress and he dices and slices his way through them. Try it next time you fancy a fruit salad — it's not as easy as they make it look — but it is a whole lot of fun.

http://y2u.be/w-llZmPPNwU

SELF ANALYSIS

What would you ask your pre-teenage self?

Jeremiah McDonald, age 12, is clever, charismatic and funny, and he also had considerable insight. Jeremiah McDonald, age 32, is also pretty smart and knows how to put a film together. And guess what? They're one and the same person! This six-minute YouTube gem was 20 years in the making, because, by means of an old VHS he made in 1992, Jeremiah has fashioned a dialogue with his young self. It works incredibly well, succeeding in being touching, funny and thought-provoking at the same time.

http://y2u.be/XFGAQrEUaeU

TOTALLY SPACED OUT

Cool experiments from outer space

You never know when you might need to wring out a wet towel in space, so this clip of a simple experiment, made by the International Space Station, could prove invaluable. Astronaut Chris Hadfield takes a compressed puck of official NASA-issue towel, squirts water over it and then wrings it out. It might sound dull, but the effect is totally cool. When you see the amazing way that water responds to zero gravity, you'll be transfixed. Budding space cadets might want to investigate more brilliant ISS videos, such as *Clipping Fingernails in Space* and *Cooking Spinach in Space*.

http://y2u.be/lMtXfwk7PXg

THIS'LL QUACK YOU UP

Cat and duck in *Jaws* remake

Sometimes the response to a viral YouTube video should just be "Why?" As in "Why on God's Earth would someone dress a cat up in a shark costume, put them on a Roomba (one of those robotic flat vacuum cleaners) and let them chase a duck around the room?" But watch this video and none of these questions will matter, because you'll just be so pleased that they bothered. And do watch all the way through — you don't want to miss the dog!

http://y2u.be/Of2HU3LGdbo

SO COOL

Are you ready to join the *Charlieissocoollike* bandwagon?

Charlie McDonnell has been posting videos on YouTube since he was 16. He's now in his mid-20s and has become one of the site's top celebrities. By posting simple, amusing blogs about his life under the name *Charlieissocoollike*, his was the first YouTube UK channel to reach one million subscribers. The cute-looking, Bieber-esque Charlie then became a star in the US when Oprah featured his *How to be English* video. This one is typically *Charlieissocoollike* as he duets with himself in his usual self-deprecating but instantly likeable way.

http://y2u.be/pVo-S9ns2_A

BEDTIME BANDIT

Kyle, the two-year-old toy thief

Kyle Moser isn't the first burglar to be caught in the act on video, but he might well be the first two-year-old. When Kyle's eight-year-old sister told her parents that her little brother was stealing things from her room at night, they told her to lock the door. She did as they suggested but still found her toys were going missing. Intrigued, the parents decided to secretly film what was happening and when Kyle ingeniously went on the hunt for a prized unicorn pillow pet, they were rewarded with a perfect 90-second crime caper.

http://y2u.be/8wk-qRfJQPM

WHO ARE YOU CALLING A ROBOT?

Eavesdropping on a conversation between talking robots

Chatbots are robots programmed to engage in human-type dialogue. They are becoming so sophisticated that they can sometimes fool people into thinking they are having a real conversation. So what happens if you put two of these bots up against each other? Will it be like one of those late-night TV arts debates? Or bons mots recalling the barbed wit of Dorothy Parker? Not wanting to give away any answers here, but listen out for the line "I am not a robot, I am a unicorn"!

http://y2u.be/WnzlbyTZsQY

CAN I HAVE MY POCKET MONEY NOW?

The sweetest duet on the web

When you think of father–daughter musical duets, names like
Frank and Nancy Sinatra, Johnny and Rosanne Cash or maybe
even Loudon and Martha Wainwright come to mind. But Jorge
Narvaez and his daughter Alexa knock the spots off them all –
because Alexa is only six years old and is as cute as a button.
Their cover of "Home" by Edward Sharpe and the Magnetic
Zeroes is enough to make even the most unsentimental of souls
melt down and weep. What's more, it earned them 25 million
views, was taken up for a Hyundai commercial and won
them a place on *America's Got Talent*.

http://y2u.be/L64c5vT3NBw

READY, STEADY ... DONE?

How quickly can you link to this page?

It's a speedster's world and don't those YouTubers know it!
Think you're quick at something? Knitting? Slicing watermelon?
Texting? Take a quick search, and you'll find someone with
superhuman skills that put your efforts to shame. Alternatively,
spend five enjoyable minutes watching a compilation of
awesome talents — a collection of speedy stuff from the world's
fastest clapper to the snappiest Rubik's Cube solver and the
quickest undresser to a record-breaking pizza maker.
Just hope your broadband speed is up to it.

http://y2u.be/k4oCrCwEIEA

DOES MY ASS LOOK BIG IN THIS?

A clip that's outstanding in its field

YouTube has cornered the market in by-passer filming. Wherever there's someone in an embarrassing situation crying out for help, there's someone else ready to stop what they are doing – and film it. The poor chap in this clip has obviously been caught short while out in the country and decided to nip into a nearby field to answer nature's call. What he couldn't have suspected is that he would arouse the interests of an over-excited donkey – or that someone would get their mobile out as he yelled for assistance.

http://y2u.be/BCcvv9D9P8M

GETTING HIGH

Let these kids test your fear of heights

When we were kids, we'd hang out in the park, maybe take in a movie or, if we were being really brave, explore the local derelict house. But these youngsters have other ideas. Their concept of a fun day out seems to be climbing out on the arm of a crane, hundreds of feet in the air. The clip is entitled *Your Hands WILL Sweat After Watching This!* and they're not wrong. It's a teeth-grindingly anxious watch, even when you've already seen it five times. And, if you suffer from vertigo, make sure you're sitting down when you try to watch.

http://y2u.be/xOlovYfgjLQ

A-MAZE-ING!

Is this the world's scariest game?

The Scary Maze Game is a YouTube phenomenon. You simply film your victim as they use their mouse to guide the cursor through an ever-more complex maze without touching the walls. On completion they are greeted with a close-up picture from the movie *The Exorcist*, along with an ear-piercing scream. Whether a hilarious prank or a mean-spirited waste of time, people persist in posting videos of their friends, family, social workers in embarrassing states of fright. Most are dull, but this is the exception – a truly, truly funny reaction.

http://y2u.be/469zNXTCHdk

WE WILL NOT LET YOU GO

When words fail you, try the lyrics of Queen

Across the world the fight for justice by those facing police charges takes many different forms. Some hire expensive lawyers to get them off the hook, others find protest groups are organized in their favour, and the less fortunate face a hard, lonely struggle. Watching this video,it appears that defendants taking issue with the police in Canada can argue their case through the performance of classic pop hits. Here Robert Wilkinson, arrested for intoxication and finding mere words insufficient, resorts to Queen's "Bohemian Rhapsody" in an impassioned plea for his release.

http://y2u.be/fqymcJRSbxl

KEEP YOUR HAIR ON

The famous homemade wig prank

Prank time again. It's giving the game away a bit, but it doesn't diminish the feel-good effect of this video from Jozaeh in Australia. He came up with the inspired idea of shaving his hair off, collecting it all up and making a wig out of it. It looks pretty authentic, good enough not to be noticed by the friends and family he gets to pose with him, but, of course, the best part is the reveal. The wonderful, if surprised, reactions to his ingenious trick have already gleaned the video two-and-a-half million views.

http://y2u.be/ZmsP2s5euhk

YOUTUBE'S SENIOR MOMENT

The oldies are still the goodies

Old people, eh? Blinking hilarious. Well, at least these two old dears are. Introducing octogenarians Bruce and Esther Huffman from McMinnville in Oregon, USA. They became unlikely YouTube celebs when their granddaughter posted a three-minute clip of their attempt to snap a photograph on their new laptop computer. It's not just about laughing at senior citizens meeting technology (fun though that is), there's also some music as Bruce stretches his vocal cords, some romance, some light bawdy suggestiveness and plenty of slapstick. At one point Esther says, "I don't know what I'm recording." Comedy gold, madam, comedy gold.

http://y2u.be/FcN08Tg3PWw

A WALK ON THE WILD SIDE

Hey, Randall, tell us all about that crazy Honey Badger

Ever watched a wildlife show and thought just how boring the
voiceover was? Struggling actor Randall thought just that and
decided to record his own narration. What made some fairly boring
footage of a badger go madly viral? Maybe his marvellously camp
delivery? Perhaps his appalled reaction to mildly gross animal
behaviour? But most probably the brilliant way he appears to
make it all up as he watches the clip. It's great to think of
David Attenborough watching in disbelief, thinking, "What,
I didn't have to fight my way into the heart of those rainforests?"

http://y2u.be/4r7wHMg5Yjg

SOMETHING A LITTLE FISHY

From market stall to Number One

Muhammad Shahid Nazir's story is a YouTube rags-to-riches fairy tale. When Nazir found a job on a fish stall at Queen's Market in East London, his boss told him he had to shout to get customers' attention. Reluctant to just yell, Nazir preferred to sing his message about the cheap seafood on sale. When a customer uploaded a video of him singing, it went viral – soon spawning a music video complete with Bollywood dancers. The song hit the charts and, despite being banned in his home country of Pakistan, turned Nazir into a global star.

http://y2u.be/ETSI8gWsFZ0

THEY'RE HUMANS JIM, BUT NOT AS WE KNOW THEM

A superb collection of extreme stunts

We're a strange race, us humans. Most of us consider getting out of the armchair a major physical accomplishment and making a cup of coffee a feat of superb dexterity. Meanwhile, it seems there's another human race whose bravery, skills and co-ordination make us look like cack-handed apes from another planet. Put together by the British band Hadouken!, whose own rocking single provides the soundtrack to *People are Awesome 2013*, this is a video which rounds up a series of mind-blowing jumps, spins, somersaults and other incredible sporting feats. Yes, maybe you should have a rest now...

http://y2u.be/A6XUVjK9W4o

SCREAM IF YOU WANT TO GO FASTER

Ride the world's scariest rollercoasters

YouTube delights in re-creating the thrills of the world's best theme-park rides. With footage captured from the actual seat, you get a pretty realistic rollercoaster trip in the comfort of your own home. However, to have a true simulation of the experience, you are welcome to: queue outside the door for an hour, give all your cash to whoever's standing around looking bored and get someone to throw a bucket of water over you at appropriate points. Still, if you are going to be sick, at least you can use a bowl rather than the hood of the person in front.

http://y2u.be/9yFvlcw8YtY

FOOTBALL FOCUS

All the action from the Binocular Soccer Cup Final

Soccer has long been searching for an alternative to penalty shoot-outs to decide tied matches. Well, what about this idea from Japan? *The Takeshi Katano Show* staged a soccer match where the players all wore binoculars that made things appear closer than they really were. You'll have to admit that, as a sport, what Binocular Soccer lacks in technical ability and goalmouth action it more than makes up for in slapstick and people-falling-over hilarity. Seriously folks, this could be the funniest clip on the whole of YouTube.

http://y2u.be/-rRK7vlBG8A

SPICING THINGS UP

That damn-fool Cinnamon Challenge

What's the dumbest craze to have ever hit YouTube? Well, the Cinnamon Challenge is certainly among the contenders. Search on those words and you'll find hundreds of would-be YouTube heroes coughing and spluttering. The challenge is simple: try to swallow a tablespoon of cinnamon in 60 seconds without any water. YouTube personality and comedienne Glozell has earned the most CC hits with this hilarious attempt – watch it and you'll quickly get the idea. However, best stick to strictly armchair viewing on this one as doctors have slapped a health warning on trying the stunt yourself.

http://y2u.be/Cyk7utV_D2l

WHEN GOOD MASCOTS GO BAD...

A compilation of sporting mascot mishaps

Who'd be a sports team's mascot? You are incarcerated in a sweat-inducing, dignity-stripping, lumbering costume for hours on end; treated with contempt by the real stars of the show; and quickly discarded by the fans when the real action starts. No wonder there seems to be a seething rage forever building under those comic features and wobbly outfits. Of course, what the punters really love is to see their mascots truly humiliated – falling flat on their grinning bug-eyed face or taking a punch from the only other poor sap in the stadium with an oversized foam-rubber head. Sit back and enjoy.

http://y2u.be/IfyJ_BqshWI

THIS CAT IS DEEP, MAN

The adventures of Henri, le Chat Noir

Henri may not be the most famous or adorable cat on the web, but he's got to be the most pretentious. His musings are delivered in captivating French, helpfully subtitled for those us whose knowledge of the language doesn't go much beyond "croissant" and "s'il vous plaît". We are thus able to glean that Henri the black cat is a tortured creature but, before you call the Cat Protection League, their literature states that unfortunately they can't do much for moggies suffering from existential angst. Definitely one for intellectuals and beret-wearers.

http://y2u.be/0M7ibPk37_U

PARALLEL UNIVERSE

The world's worst attempt at parking

Perhaps it was just one of those nightmares where frustration, despair and humiliation seem on a never-ending loop. Could it really have taken this Belfast woman a full half-an-hour to park in a space large enough to leave a bus? Was there really a gaggle of incredibly irritating students watching, jeering and cheering her every — and there were many — attempt to reverse into the space? Did they really post it on YouTube where it went viral and attracted media interest around the world? Oh yes, yes and yes. And very funny it is too!

http://y2u.be/tf4TIWECZ30

THE BESTEST ... YUMMA!

She forgot the blueberries – or did she?

Recipe time. Take one shaky camera and an ordinary kitchen.
Now add a sweet child eager to make a sensible video on how to
make a fruit salad and leave to stand for 20 seconds. Then pour
in a younger sister, very excitable, not quite as sensible, but still
equally sweet. Mix the ingredients until fabulous comic moments
rise to the surface. Upload in the YouTube oven and leave to
go viral. Other versions, parodies and remixes are available,
but none tastes half as good as the original.

http://y2u.be/yqEeP1acj4Y

I GOT THOSE CAN'T-PLAY-THE-GUITAR BLUES

He's a guitarist and he's mighty angry

First of all a warning – this video is full of swearing, but it's far too funny to leave out, so if you're easily offended or a minor, mute your sound and watch it anyway. This is all you need to know: the Treeman hails from Liverpool. His attempts to play guitar have made him a global YouTube star, but for all the wrong reasons. The Treeman is known as "the angriest guitar player in the world" because, when he gets something wrong, he loses it completely and takes out his anger on the nearest person and object – himself and his guitar!

http://y2u.be/Vms_6_TSQuc

YOU'RE ALL THE MEME

Their part in Hitler's *Downfall*

Every now and then YouTube will remake a video to death. Such was the fate of the parodies of *Downfall*, the movie of Hitler's last days, in which the subtitles were changed to suit every kind of rant from Disney buying Marvel to sub-prime mortgages. They were, and still can be, very witty. Run through the list and you might find one that suits your own sporting or political cause, but to pick one that sums up the meme is easy. Here, Herr Hitler's tirade concerns the *Downfall* parodies getting out of hand on YouTube. Clever, eh!

http://y2u.be/ChEXf91j2pU

BABY BOOMER

You're familiar with Iron Man – now meet "Iron Baby"

Parodies of the blockbuster movie *Iron Man* are a popular YouTube meme. He's been remade in cardboard, recast in Thailand and been hilariously "honested" (search for *Honest Trailers*), but this one – with that special "cute baby" ingredient – went way-out viral. The two-year-old is fabulously suited-up for bad-guy action, but quite how his parents are going to fare when it's time for a bottom clean-up is anyone's guess. And the way he deals with those evil bunnies makes you fear for mum and dad's lives when they tell him it's time for bed.

http://y2u.be/GaaQwJAww6s

BATMAN LIVES!

Jeb Corliss – the Amazing Flying Man

Jeb's idea of fun is putting on a tiny bat suit and jumping off cliffs, mountains and tall buildings. The most famous BASE jumper in the world, Jeb Corliss has leapt from the Eiffel Tower and the Space Needle and is banned from going near the Empire State Building. Strapped with a camera, he has the most magnificent collection of YouTube videos as he glides through the air at speeds of around 120mph. *Grinding the Crack* is his exhilarating ride through a Swiss gorge but check out *Grounded* if you want to see what happens when it all goes – literally – belly up.

http://y2u.be/TWfph3iNC-k

WALK THIS WAY

The amazing Japanese synchronized walking show

Who would believe that watching people walking could be quite
so side-splittingly hilarious, but this is among the most bizarre
and, in a strange way, fantastic videos out there. You've heard
of synchronized swimmers with their impressive underwater
routines, but synchronized walking takes things to another level.
At first you might think it's just a military-style marching show,
but, oh no – these guys have more in their artillery than strolling
up and down – stick with it and you are in for a treat. I bet you'll
soon be signing the petition to make it an Olympic sport.

http://y2u.be/E7cQtbMtODk

DAT WAZ AWESOME!

It's always a good idea to finish with some fireworks

If you are not keen on profanities or blasphemous language, it might be worth giving this one a miss, but you'll be forgoing 60 seconds of panic-stricken delight. Perhaps this works because we've all been there – watching a situation get out of hand and being unable to do anything but voice your fears in exclamations and appeals to the Almighty – but, as a YouTube video, it is completely perfect. It features an exciting incident, steady camera work, fabulous commentary and perfect subtitles – with the "Jesus!" counter as the icing on the cake!

http://y2u.be/NRItYDKSqpQ

A RIGHT CHARLIE

Possibly the most famous home video in the world

Charlie Bit My Finger – Again! is just a sweet, short film of
two boys which any family would cherish. Perhaps, in years to
come, the parents might retrieve it and shed a nostalgic tear or
embarrass the boys in front of their girlfriends but, in uploading
it for the English boys' relatives in the USA, their father
inadvertently launched the most-viewed non-professional music
video on YouTube. Just what the magic ingredient is – the baby's
knowing look, the almost old-fashioned English accent,
or the earnest remonstrations – is a matter for discussion
but, if you could bottle it, you'd never need to work again...

http://y2u.be/_OBlgSz8sSM

MY DAD'S A SUPERHERO

Nana, nana, nana, nana...

He's YouTube's very own superhero; a parenting vigilante, whose authentic-sounding, gravelly voiced diktats rule the roost in his family. When father of four Blake Wilson dons his Batman mask, his family sit up and listen (OK, maybe his wife wears a slightly "not again" expression). Whether he's dishing out on table manners, dental hygiene, wearing safety belts or bedtime routines, it's performed with immaculate timing and great humour. Just one note of caution: anyone else get the feeling that his light-hearted warnings and rebukes might not go down quite so well once those kids become sullen, hypersensitive teenagers?

http://y2u.be/YlVi0noRr-o

BIEBER BUNNY BOILER

The rise and rise of the over-attached girlfriend

Not since the movie *Fatal Attraction* has a stalker made for such good entertainment. When Justin Bieber ran a competition for devoted female fans to submit "girlfriend" versions of his hit single "Boyfriend", Laina Walker grabbed her opportunity – but maybe not in the way Justin expected. Playing on the "needy" side of Bieber's song, Laina portrays an insanely jealous stalker-girlfriend brilliantly, with awesomely creepy intensity, incredible staring ability and hilarious lyrics. Laina has since become a YouTube celebrity, clocking up another hit with a "Call Me Maybe" parody and earning herself a major advertising contract.

http://y2u.be/Bqa-C4EbGqo

"A STUPID FOX SONG"

I think we all know what he says by now, thank you...

Norwegian comedy duo Ylvis claimed the top-trending video of 2013. Brothers Vegard and Bård Ylvisåker produced the video to promote their TV series, but soon found themselves with a global hit on their hands (paws?) as it took just 35 days to hit 100 million views. Even Bård called it "a stupid Fox song", but damn, it's catchy — acha-chacha-chacha-chow! Of course, it led to hundreds of parodies, some better than others, with perhaps the best being *What Does the Spleen Do?* by Harvard Medical School students.

http://y2u.be/jofNR_WkoCE

UNICORNS OF THE SEA

Doner miss this whale of a tribute

It is about time YouTube took notice of the narwhal – the fabled unicorn of the sea. For far too long these majestic two-toothed inhabitants of Arctic waters have been uncelebrated on the web's prime site. OK, maybe Weebl, the producers of this catchy ditty, have gone a little over the top (are these whales really the Jedi of the sea?), and included some details David Attenborough might dispute (could they really beat a polar bear in a fight?), and are possibly just lying (did they really invent the shish kebab?), but the similarly unserenaded jelly fish would doubtless love to be honoured with such an awesome animation.

http://y2u.be/ykwqXuMPsoc

FREE YOUR INNER HORSE

Time to saddle up? Please say no – or should that be neigh?

Looking to get fit? Ready to get sweaty? Not afraid to look a
complete idiot in front of the world? Then prancercise could
be for you. This brand-new dance/exercise, invented by Joanna
Rohrback, mimics the movements of a horse – galloping,
trotting and that strange head-bobbing thing. When the
YouTube video went viral in 2013, many were left to ponder
if this could be the new aerobics. Or were people just having
a good laugh at a weird-looking woman who walks like
there's something seriously wrong with her?

http://y2u.be/o-50GjySwew

McFLY ME TO THE MOON

Boybander Tom Fletcher sings his wedding speech

It's that part of the wedding everyone dreads. The groom stands, reaches for his notes and you brace yourself for an hour of excruciating boredom, endless thank-yous and having to laugh at feeble jokes. But not for the lucky guests at the wedding of McFly's Tom Fletcher. For Tom decided to sing his speech, changing the words of his band's greatest hits to pay tribute to his new wife, her parents, the ushers etc, etc, etc... Sounds dreadful? Gushing, pretentious and embarrassing? Well, actually, it isn't. It's well-performed, perfectly judged and, go on, admit it, touching.

http://y2u.be/27WufdasQYs

FIRE, POLICE, AMBULANCE ... SIR ALEX FERGUSON?

Of course it's an emergency – United lost!

When is an emergency an emergency and when is it just an unfortunate and rather embarrassing situation? Many of us have experienced that dilemma. Is that my teenage son climbing into next door's window or an intruder? Can I ease the toddler's head out of the park railings or is oxyacetylene equipment needed? Do I have bubonic plague or is it just bad acne? Should I call the emergency services or not? On such occasions, this is the kind of bloke you want around. He doesn't demur. He doesn't dither. He's decisive. Manchester United, one of the world's biggest football teams, are having a mediocre season, so he calls 999.

http://y2u.be/S24JXYLswc0

MAKING MILEY LOOK PANTS

Wrecking the wrecking ball

YouTube has no qualms about members posting the best of other social video networks, so increasingly we find videos crossing over from Vine, Vimeo and, in this case, Chatroulette. The amazing success of Miley Cyrus's videos provoked many parodies, but clad in Y-fronts and a vest, Steve Kardynal gives it his all. His split-screen Chatroulette followers watch in amazement, hilarity, disbelief and shock as bearded Steve dutifully hammers and writhes on his home-made wrecking ball. His spoof video received over nine million views in 24 hours, surpassing the views received by Miley's own performance of the song at the 2013 American Music Awards.

http://y2u.be/W6DmHGYy_xk

DAWG! LOOK AT HIM GO!

Tillman — the most famous dog on wheels

In 2009, Tillman the English bulldog set a world record for the fastest 100m canine skateboard, covering the distance in 19.678 seconds. These days, "Pot Roast", as he's nicknamed, is a celebrity dog. He's a TV star with his own Facebook page and it really would be no surprise to find him hanging around bus stops in baggy shorts and Vans. Tillman's talents and rise to fame are well chronicled on YouTube. Let's just hope he doesn't get hooked on chews, start paying for visits from bitches and begin endless visits to canine rehab.

http://y2u.be/DO3Awc2lo1k

DYING TO SEE YOU

The strangest – and best – ever safety warning

What kind of safety advice would recommend using your private parts as piranha bait? Only the funniest and most entertaining thing to come out of Australia since Harold Bishop left *Neighbours*. Those advertising folk can be pretty clever. Tasked to come up with a safety message to warn kids about fooling around near train tracks, the agency devised a multi-award-winning animation. It draws you in with a beautifully sung catchy ditty and a series of adorable, colourful cartoon blob characters, before hitting you with some gruesome – if amusing – words and images. Nothing short of YouTube genius.

http://y2u.be/IJNR2EpS0jw

JUST HOBBIT OF FUN

Elvishly yours...

Here's the choice. You could sit through 30 hours of *The Lord of the Rings* trilogy and follow the seemingly endless adventures of Benbo Bodkins and his merry band of leprechauns – or you could give up two minutes of your time to enjoy this piece of YouTube frippery. You'll get the beautiful scenery, Orlando Bloom, some endearing little creatures and a jolly tune to hum along to. No contest. And fair play to the lead man: seek out *Orlando Bloom "They're Taking the Hobbits to Isengard" Live* and see the film's star enjoying a laugh-along, sing-along version.

http://y2u.be/bZ2oWNsVt38

AWW! WE'VE STILL GOT IT!

Yep – a year on and humans are still awesome

Awesomeness? It's all relative, right? You might think
getting your history assignment in on time was a pretty good
achievement for the year, right? But British band Hadouken!
looked for something a little more exciting for the follow-up to
their 2012 viral video hit *People are Awesome*. To the soundtrack
of "Levitate", one of the band's catchy indie-pop songs, we get
some of the best of YouTube's jumpers, divers and somersaulters
– with the odd daredevil lunatic stunt thrown in here and there.
Fabulously edited and with real gobsmacking feats,
it's worth interrupting your homework to watch.

http://y2u.be/A6XUVjK9W4o

EXTREME WAKE-UP CALL

Ghostly goings-on in perfect prank

"I wanted to see how my girlfriend would react to a ghost coming out the TV trying to grab hold of her." Of course he did. It's not enough for James Williams to make scary noises from behind the sofa or jump out of the wardrobe as she goes to choose a dress. James really, really, really wants to frighten her out of her skin. So, replicating a scene from horror film *The Ring*, he builds a realistic, life-size, papier-mâché ghost. While his girlfriend is sleeping, James clamps it to the TV, before waking her with a ghostly howl. Amazingly, the couple are still together.

http://y2u.be/UEnyJxaxTp8

UNIVERSITY CHALLENGE!

The most inspirational speech ever!

Next time your teacher, boss, sports coach or parents try to motivate you with some carefully chosen and well-rehearsed words, just fire this up and show them how it should be done. Nicholas Selby, a student at Georgia Institute of Technology, took up the challenge of welcoming new students to the university in Atlanta and produced what some have called the most inspirational speech ever. He does make it sound a great place. Wonder what grades you need?

http://y2u.be/98nNpzE6gls

CALL AND (NO) RESPONSE

Boom, boom, boom — everybody say ... huh?

Hey guys, remember the Outthere Brothers? No? "Boom, Boom, Boom"? Still nothing? Well, never mind. It was a UK hit in 1995 and had a funky beat and a shout-out chorus. They say, "Let me hear you say 'way-ho'." You say, "Way-ho." Somehow, this song became quite a YouTube anthem. Norwegian teenager Catherine Marjorie Solumsmo clocked up most hits with her somewhat understated version on *CathyMay15 Boom Boom Boom Way Ho Girl*. But this is more fun, as Stuart Moffat tests out just who does remember the legendary ditty. Not many, then...

http://y2u.be/FuleTVQ5EoY

3D OR NOT 3D

Introducing the anamorphic optical illusion

This'll freak you out, but in an intriguing, mind-bending, nice way. We're talking anamorphic optical illusions here, which means that, at one particular angle, an image appears to be three-dimensional, but move your position and the whole thing distorts and changes. It's dead clever but basically an ancient art trick practised by the likes of Michaelangelo. Brasspup films some perfect examples using household items such as Rubik's Cubes and trainers. He even gives you links to print them out and try them yourself. Watch out for that cat, though!

http://y2u.be/tBNHPk-Lnkk

MARCHING POWER

Better than a half-time pie and a Bovril

If you think that pimply faced teenagers walking up and down playing trombones and drums at half-time is boring, take a look at this mob. Their Disney Tribute show was pretty impressive and their Video Games performance was gobsmacking, but then they took it up a level. Their Hollywood Blockbusters show, featuring tunes from *Superman, Lord of the Rings, Harry Potter, Jurassic Park* and *Pirates of the Caribbean*, is an awesome display of creative, er, marching up and down. Their performances really are impressive they're not nicknamed "The Best Damn Band in the Land" for nothing.

http://y2u.be/DNeOZUD19EE

MARRIED BLISS

A gorgeous nurse turns out to be his wife

Ready for a little heart-warming gooeyness? And this time there's not a cat, dog or animated creature in sight. Meet Jason Mortensen. He's coming round after a hernia operation and is still feeling a little groggy. Fortunately, a nurse is on hand to check he's OK and feed him a cracker. More fortunate still, she has the foresight to film the unfolding events. That's because the "nurse" is about to reveal to Jason that she is actually his wife. How does he react? Get the tissues ready!

http://y2u.be/IqebEymqFS8

KILLER TIME

Do you have a question for a cold-blooded assassin?

What do you know about ninja? You may be aware that they wear headbands, practise lethal martial arts and are deadly assassins. Those who have studied them might tell you they can be killed only by another ninja and that they can scale walls effortlessly. But what if you need to know more? Look no further than YouTube's *Ask a Ninja*. Here, you can discover if ninjas catch colds, what gift to give a ninja and how to play "niniature golf". But be careful out there. Don't get too near the screen — behind each answer is a ninja just looking for a killing.

http://y2u.be/qdS5lkeN8_8

QUITE LITERALLY BEAUTIFUL

Music video that tells it like it is

YouTube's "literal" craze has produced some witty and clever videos. You may already have seen the A-Ha "Take on Me" literal, where the lyrics are changed to reflect what actually happens in the video. In James Blunt's "You're Beautiful", James gets cold in the rain and that's about it, but we're treated to great lines like, "Now you're going to see my chest". If you're hooked on literals, you could also check out "Never Going to Give You Up" by the web's favourite figure of fun, Rick Astley.

http://y2u.be/YOII5Qiq-9g

TIME TRAVEL

Take a trip through the streets of London – past and present

Cinematographer Claude Friese-Greene's celebrated film *The Open Road* is a series of silent travelogues of Britain made to promote his late father's pioneering colour-film process. In 1927 he completed filming the streets of London, capturing some fabulous images of the city. Now for the clever bit: in 2013 filmmaker Simon Smith followed his footsteps, filming exactly the same streets of the capital. How much has changed in the intervening 86 years? You might be surprised.

http://y2u.be/N8IXzSCOFZQ

ETCH-A-SKETCH

The animated comedy kings of YouTube

YouTube really is a world of its own and ASDF (Ass-Duff-Moo-Vee) are aristocracy. This series of simple but very funny cartoon animations by TomSka has notched up an amazing 100 million hits. Clever, random and zany, each video is made up of a number of sketches played out in distinctive line drawings, each lasting about 10 seconds. There's a pretty high hit-to-miss ratio of gags, visual jokes and slapstick, and the one-liners can be fabulous, but watch out — you won't be the only one repeating them in the office or playground.

http://y2u.be/CU0vWXKetec

216

TUBE TRAINING

Moscow subway squats

As if travelling by tube train isn't already enough of an assault
course – fighting for a space on the platform, jostling for elbow
room in the carriage and climbing hundreds of steps because the
escalator is broken – the Moscow system offered passengers the
choice of doing 30 squats in order to get a free ticket. Of course,
you can choose to pay for your ticket and avoid the humiliation
of getting on the train red-faced, sweaty and out of breath.
What do you mean, you look like that anyway?

http://y2u.be/qaPNDbGKr7k

HE SAID WHAT?!

What the stars of American football are talking about

The Bad Lip Reading channel really took off during the 2012 US Presidential Election campaign, when its sometimes hilarious, sometimes bizarre, but always incorrect lip-reading interpretations went viral. But the anonymous genius who puts these together surpassed him- or herself with this fabulous collection of American-football heroes and their misquotes. Look out for the Orange Peanut... classic.

http://y2u.be/Zce-QT7MGSE

WHEN IN ROME...

Three tenors for the price of one

It was the eve of the 1990 FIFA World Cup Final in Rome. With
Britain still coping with the trauma of Gazza's tears at going out
in the semi-final, the three greatest singers on the planet took to
the stage to wring out the last bit of emotion left in the country.
José Carreras, Luciano Pavarotti and Plácido Domingo (Homer
Simpson's "third favourite" of the Three Tenors) came together in
the ruins of ancient Rome to perform. Such was the reaction that
the recording became the best-selling classical record ever and
"Nessun Dorma" became a somewhat unlikely football anthem.

http://y2u.be/r8MbJAU8hDohttp

HELL NO!

Quiet night in

If you're one of those horror-movie watchers who constantly screams, "Why on earth would he go in there?" or, "Why don't you just call the cops?" or even, "Why a remote cabin in a dark wood? What's wrong with the Travelodge?" then *Hell No! The Sensible Horror Movie* is for you. Here are horror-film trailers where the characters make the right decisions. No gore, no goose bumps and certainly no flesh-eating zombies, just a lot of common sense.

http://y2u.be/Sq9m9u7loxM

THROWING THE BIG ONE

It's not fair! It's the greatest temper tantrum ever!

Your little brother thinks he's making a point as he slams the door and shouts, "I wish I'd never been born," then storms off to his bedroom to sulk. But he's got a fair way to go before he's even in the same league as Stephen Quire. Admittedly, the teenager has been viciously provoked. His mum has just cancelled his World of Warcraft account. Who wouldn't fly off the handle? Unfortunately, he also has a cruel elder brother who's set up to film the whole thing – the threats to run away, the hyperventilating and that strange thing with the remote.

http://y2u.be/YerslyzsOpc

SOME CAFFEINE BUZZ!

The telekinetic coffee shop surprise

The corporate promotional prank race continues to evolve and the videos get ever more elaborate. This stunning stunt for the remake of the horror classic *Carrie* sets the bar pretty high. Over 50 million people have clicked on to watch the fall-out when a teenage girl freaks out over her flat white getting knocked over. We've already seen the preparation for the stunt, but the expression on the faces of the unsuspecting customers at a New York City coffee shop as the girl unleashes her "telekinetic powers" is utterly priceless. Just a shame that the movie turned out to be such a farmyard turkey!

http://y2u.be/VlOxlSOr3_M

UNLEASH YOUR INNER BABY

Mini-me mirror dancing

Evian's roller-skating-babies ad set the record for the most-viewed online advertisement (over 170 million views) in 2009, so they needed to follow it up with something pretty special. Did they manage it? Well, they stuck to the same formula, found another nostalgia dance hit (Ini Kamoze's "Here Comes the Hotstepper") and brought in some dancing babies, this time mirror dancing to their lookalike adult selves. Quite what the whole thing has to do with bottled water is anyone's guess, but there's no doubt they've found themselves another hit – you'll watch it again and again.

http://y2u.be/pfxB5ut-KTs

TAKING THE RAP

It's the contest of the century: Mozart vs Skrillex

Nice Peter and Lloyd Ahlquist's hilarious rap battles have carved out a well-deserved niche in the YouTube community. Their boasting and insulting-in-rhyme competitions pit celebrities and historical and fictional figures against each other in two-minute bouts. Witty, imaginative and funny, they have become increasingly well produced since the early battles, such as Darth Vader versus Adolf Hitler. Other classic matches pit Mario Bros up against the Wright Bros and find Genghis Khan scrapping it out with the Easter Bunny, but this has to be a favourite, if only for the classic line, "I've seen more complexity in a couch from Ikea."

http://y2u.be/_6AuOxCg3PI

CHOLESTEROL DAMAGE

Everything you shouldn't eat – in one epic meal

You've had your five-a-day fruit, a small salad and downed your ginseng yin-yang juice, but still feel a little peckish?

How about a recipe from the Epic Meal Time boys? These bacon-loving Canadian 20-somethings have gained notoriety concocting feasts that will have your arteries shrieking in fear. One-time substitute teacher Harley Morenstein and his gang use ingredients as diverse as waffles, cake mix, tortilla chips, maple syrup, fast food items, Baileys, cheese sticks and pounds and pounds of bacon. Their fast food pizza notched up 286g (10oz) of fat and 5,210 calories, but this gourmet delight exceeds even that!

http://y2u.be/jXjxHQQxcLw

HIT THE GROUND RUNNING

The incredible fate of the skydiving camera

A skydiver's helmet-mounted camera comes loose and falls out of the plane just as the diver is ready to jump. The camera drops all the way to the ground and, putting it down to bad luck, the diver gets on with his adrenaline-pumping life. Fast-forward eight months and a farmer comes across a camera. When he checks out the contents of its memory, he is amazed... and so will you be. This extraordinary accidental video captures the camera's spinning adventure and even has its own fabulous and surprising ending.

http://y2u.be/QrxPuk0JefA

MOVIE STAR CEREAL KILLER

Ryan Gosling won't eat his breakfast

If you want to create a successful Internet meme, your best bet is to hit on Hollywood star Ryan Gosling. The Internet just loves any Gosling-based fun. *Hey Girl* saw sultry Ryan uttering nauseating pick-up lines, *Feminist Ryan Gosling* gave his pronouncements a political bent and, in *Ryan Gosling Breaks Up a Fight in New York,* he does just that – what a hero! But there's something about Ryan refusing his cereal that tops the lot. Producer Ryan McHenry offers up spoonfuls of cornflakes at moments of intense drama and elicits some – unintentional – hilarious responses from the hunky actor.

http://y2u.be/jxs791pjOeg

CLASSROOM DROP-OFF

Detention for the drowsy duckling?

This is a situation that will have most of us sympathizing. You've had a tough morning followed by a nice lunch and are just about ready for a little afternoon nap. Then the bell goes and you're due back in the classroom. It doesn't matter how scintillating your teacher is, that dozy feeling just won't go away. So, here we are in an Australian college, listening to a lesson in accountancy and one poor chap – OK, it's the cutest of ducklings – just can't seem to stay awake. And trying to get up and leave proves an even worse idea. Just cuter than cute!

http://y2u.be/LGrpsZ7BsQA

WHOSE BED IS IT ANYWAY?

Who said anything about letting sleeping cats lie?

Since the great Treaty of Barking in the late twentieth century, cats and dogs have maintained a reasonably harmonious relationship in domestic households around the world. But word is creeping out that the feline side is taking advantage of the non-aggression pact. This smuggled-out collection of videos is intended to alert the world's dogs to the bitter struggle being enacted. While the cats are by turn proud, smug, unabashed and downright inflammatory, the canines are singularly frustrated and powerless. "They're taking our beds now," they complain. "How much provocation do we have to take?"

http://y2u.be/Dod2VzUFNW0

HIGH-HANDED ARREST

The most eloquent and gentlemanly drunkard ever

Filmed in 1988, but a recent arrival on YouTube, this gem stars former chef Paul Charles Dozsa being shoved into a police car after pulling his "dine and dash" trick: ordering an expensive meal at a hotel, tucking in, then claiming he can't afford to pay. But Dozsa steals the show by being the most eloquent and gentlemanly drunkard ever to be manhandled (and he really is *man*handled) by the boys in blue. His outrage, protestations and language went viral and can't fail to raise a smile — even if you've seen it before.

http://y2u.be/pEsZkTTgydc

PIGLETMOBILE

Whee! Whee! Whee! All the way home

This little piggy was dropped off at a vet's in Florida, the owner expecting his cute little porker to be put down. For the little piglet, just 10 days old and weighing only 450g (1lb), had been born without the use of his hind legs. However, the vet, Len Lucero, had other ideas. Using a kid's construction toy, he set about building a wheelchair for the winsome little grunter, whom he named Chris P. Bacon. Chris seems to have taken to his mobility vehicle and you could say he's as happy as a pig on wheels!

http://y2u.be/4Z-uO5TPQfM

OLD DOG, NEW TRICKS

He's not called Jumpy for nothing...

This four-and-a-half-year-old border collie could just be the most talented mutt in the world. OK, he does the expected – the back-flipping Frisbee-catching, the surfing, the skateboarding and the slalom-running – but Jumpy has a whole host in his repertoire, some of them simply incredible. Just watch him go! And he can do charming, too. Indeed, with a wink and a modest paw over his face, Jumpy appears to be a better actor than many of his human Hollywood counterparts. Want to see more of Jumpy? Search for *Bad Ass Dog 2+*.

http://y2u.be/5l_QzPLEjM4

SQUEAK UP LITTLE GUY

The most adorable frog in the world

It had to happen eventually. For years, YouTube has bombarded us with adorable kitties, bewitching mutts, sneezing pandas and dramatic chipmunks, but now an amphibian has joined the parade – and what a little cutie it is, too. This is a desert rain frog but it actually resembles a plastic dog-chew toy. It even makes an endearing squeak, which we are informed is its "war cry". However, don't be deceived – this brutal killer can leap up to 2.5m (8ft) and take your ear off with a single bite. Just kidding! Awwww! Look at its little sandy rump.

http://y2u.be/cBkWhkAZ9ds

EASTLEIGH'S GOT TALENT

Do the bus stop shuffle

It's even worse than George Orwell predicted in *1984*. Not only is our every move being monitored by CCTV cameras, but now everyone is a talent spotter and we're all auditioning. There was a time when you could pick your nose, scratch your backside or adjust your pants in public. But no longer. Take Ellie Cole from Eastleigh, Hampshire. She was just waiting for a bus and bopping along to Alesha Dixon's "Knock Down" on her headphones. The next thing she knows, she's gone viral as the Dancing Queen of the Bus Stop. Heaven help us all!

http://y2u.be/I0mmVPV4w7c

FATHER'S DAY

Schoolboy's day of reckoning

We'll leave this one to Aria Shahrokhshahi, the lad who set up a camera to film his dad's reaction to his news: "Hey there, everyone, the man in the video is my dad. One year before this video I was a grade F in maths and in England you need a C [pass] to basically do anything with your life. I've never been amazing academically and have struggled throughout school..." If you want to see the opposite reaction, find *Irish Father's Priceless Reaction After Son Pretends to Fail*.

http://y2u.be/Ls9Cg8iaq1s

MATCH OF THE DAY

Strike a light! It's a slow-mo match head

You strike a match. It ignites and burns, until you do that panicky shaking thing when your fingers get too hot. That's about it for most of us, but by shooting a match head at 4,000 frames per second, the Ultra-Slo Studio team reveal the whole process in amazing detail. Taking a couple of minutes to even get to the flame, we see, in super-close-up, the chemical reaction that results in fire. Even if you're not interested in the science, it's a bewitching couple of minutes' viewing.

http://y2u.be/_074G_bk5sY

MAXIMUM DPH (DUMBNESS PER HOUR)

Because there's maths, applied maths, pure maths and plain wrong maths

On a road trip to Boise, Idaho, Travis Chambers asked his wife Chelsea a simple maths question: if you're travelling at 80 miles per hour, how long does it take you to go 80 miles? She tried to work it out in her head, he posted her four-minute response, and soon it was registering millions of hits. As her complex calculations went viral, Travis even left a comment: "This is not going to be easy to break to my wife." Just how long does it take a humiliated spouse to throw a tablet across a room, then?

http://y2u.be/Qhm7-LEBznk

TRICK AND TREAT

The amazing Halloween stick kid

Ah, those scary Halloween kids. They come knocking at your
door with greased-back hair and some plastic fangs and you're
expected to dish out fistfuls of Haribos. But if you met Zoe down
a dark alley, I bet your heart would miss a beat or two. Zoe's dad,
Royce Hutain, of Huntington Beach, California, made the toddler
an LED suit, transforming her into a ghostly walking stick figure.
Cute and scary in one outfit — you can just guess how
brimful her little bucket was that night.

http://y2u.be/GkBDRUO8hAo

EXTREME PREJUDICE

Some of my best friends are...

Fortunately, racism rarely rears its ugly head on YouTube but, hopefully, on this occasion you'll forgive its appearance because this video is very, very funny. The news reporter, it seems, is on the trail of a highly controversial story. An Aussie householder has placed a classified ad announcing the sale of his house with the stipulation, "No Asians". The reporter and his news crew manage to corner him in front of the property, determined to hold him to account. His explanation isn't exactly what they expected...

http://y2u.be/0YM9Ereg2Zo

HAPPY FEET

Street soccer flicks and tricks bring Internet hits

When you were a kid you might have called it "keepie-uppie", but they've now made a sport of it and it's known as "freestyle football". It's actually a collection of incredibly skilful and jaw-dropping moves – think of a show-off version of Cristiano Ronaldo (OK, maybe that doesn't work). Anyway, meet Arnaud "Séan" Garnier and his incredible array of fancy footwork. He demonstrates his art amid some busy crowds but you can't help wondering how he'd fare against a hefty centre-back clogger on a wet night in Grimsby.

http://y2u.be/yxQHgVhxfMc

CAN'T TASE THIS!

Student in most embarrassing stun gun appeal ever

This clip, taken from a dull 2007 speech by US Senator
John Kerry at the University of Florida, launched a phrase
that has appeared in songs, TV episodes, ring tones and on
T-shirts. It's not the dreary Kerry who says it, though, but earnest
student Andrew Meyer, who found out that only senators
can get away with being truly dull. As his own stultifying
contribution to the debate is met by police wielding their
favourite toy gun, Meyer shrieks his homeboy plea. It
didn't take long for YouTubers to work their magic.

http://y2u.be/QkkLUP-gm4Q

SPLIT PERSONALITY

Jean-Claude in epic truck-to-truck stunt

Two trucks, the Muscles from Brussels and an awesome sunset was all it took (in just one take, according to the producers) to send this Volvo ad into the viral stratosphere. Whether or not you take in the whole "pair of legs engineered to defy the laws of physics" spiel or the Volvo precision steering message, it's a pretty impressive 90 seconds' work. Of course, these hard men being what they are, it wasn't long before it was challenged. Chuck Norris, indeed, produced a pretty funny parody in *Greetings From Chuck Norris (the Epic Christmas Split)*.

http://y2u.be/M7Flvfx5J10

BIG SPLASH!

Tom Daley has something he wants to say…

Tom Daley was Britain's 2012 Olympic pin-up boy. As the photogenic teenager high-dived his way to a bronze medal, he was swooned over by millions of young girls (as well as their mums and quite a few guys). It's difficult enough for any sportsperson to admit to a gay relationship, but Tom also had a highly marketable boyband-like status to jeopardize. His YouTube "statement", uploaded in December 2013, was not only brave but touchingly delivered as he demonstrated his pride and conviction in such an upbeat, honest and heartwarming fashion.

http://y2u.be/OJwJnoB9EKw

SOMETHING FISHY

TED illuminates the magic of the deep sea

If you have a few minutes to fill, head for YouTube's fascinating collection of TED Talks. TED stands for Technology, Entertainment and Design, and its mini-lectures by the world's leading thinkers and doers cover these topics as well as science, business, politics and the arts. This one is a favourite – oceanographer David Gallo's entertaining talk and jaw-dropping footage of amazing deep-sea creatures, including a shape-shifting cuttlefish, a pair of fighting squid and a mesmerizing gallery of bioluminescent fish that light up the blackest depths of the ocean.

http://y2u.be/YVvn8dpSAt0

WHICH DIRECTION?

Boyband in existentialist thriller?

Why would anyone want to have a poke at One Direction? The talented lads with a penchant for harmonies and wispy hair have built a reputation for their sensitive pop pap. But suddenly, online wags Bad Lip Reading have turned the boys into laughing stock by making them the stars of a new foreign arthouse film, *Shadow Pico*. This faux movie trailer, set to the video for the song "Gotta Be You" — all meaningful looks and heartfelt confrontations — is pure gibberish and absolute comedy gold.

http://y2u.be/MYNJwpHWsBg

BEAM ME UP, SCOTTY

Star Trek encounters planet twerk

As soon as Miley and young-ish Robin foisted their twerk upon a wholly suspecting world, the race was on for the best parody. This fabulous mash-up set a pretty high standard. Yep, Captain Kirk, Uhuru, Checkov et al. have seen some pretty horrific stuff on their viewscreen, but what they're about to see will put all those aliens in the shade, although thankfully, we're spared the "where no man has been before" comments. For *Breaking Bad* fans, *Hank and Marie Watch Miley Cyrus at the VMAs* is a highly recommended runner-up.

http://y2u.be/k6Lb3kFwJRQ

JUST KIDDING AROUND

Because goats just wanna have fun

"Chèvres en équilibre" might sound like a pretentious arty French film from the 1960s, but it's actually one of the best minutes of footage to be uploaded to YouTube in the last couple of years. It translates as "goats balancing" and is just that. Three young goats climb and attempt to stay on a flexible sheet of metal. It's a fabulous playground ride for the farmyard trio, watched over by their tethered elder, who gives them a friendly butt every time they jump or fall off. It's innocent, fun and totally, totally captivating.

http://y2u.be/58-atNakMWw

CUPBOARD LOVE

The little lad who tells it like it is

The things you get forced to do when you're a cute little toddler. Go on – tell the nice man what you said to mummy again. Yeah, OK, if it means I'll get something decent to eat. This little chap came up with one little gem of homespun honesty and you can bet it's going to stay with him for years to come. He's already been "made" to repeat his famous sentence over 100 million times online and probably still enjoys the fame. But just wait until he's 14 and his classmates discover his little party piece...

http://y2u.be/E8aprCNnecU

EPIC BEAUTORIAL FAIL

It's enough to make your hair curl

This hilarious two-minute video combines two of YouTube's duller obsessions to create one crazy viral. The number of "epic fail" videos featuring slipping, tripping, blundering idiots is matched only by the volume of beauty tutorials posted by spotty teenagers who have learned to wield an eye pencil. So, step forward Tori Locklear to demonstrate both fads at once. Earnest Tori is itching to bring a little more glamour to the world with an online lesson on how to use a hair-curling iron. Now, let me get this right: I've wrapped my hair in the iron... I've counted to 20... oh-my-god!

http://y2u.be/LdVuSvZOqXM

MUPPETS 11

Muppetational *Oceans 11* movie mash-up

This is a fun game. Take two films that have nothing in common and, with a little editing and redubbing of voices, create a trailer for a brand-new movie. A kids' movie can become a horror nightmare or a rom-com can turn into a tense thriller. Sometimes it works spectacularly well and sometimes, well, it looks like two films spliced together. This one cleverly puts together the voices of *Oceans 11* and scenes from *The Muppets*, but you could also check out *Ninja Turtles/Reservoir Dogs*, *You Got Served/Wizard of Oz* or the fabulously titled *Brokeback to the Future*.

http://y2u.be/O1Q7f-fPXcM

BUZZ LIKES BIG BUTTS

"Baby Got Back" as sung by the movies

YouTuber dondrapersayswhat describes his video pretty simply.
"Clips from 295 movies used to recreate Sir Mix-A-Lot's 'Baby Got
Back' – because I'm just that much of a nerd." Whatever inspired
him to use the 1992 hit, which begins, "I like big butts and I
cannot lie," isn't made clear, but the musical mash-up is genius,
featuring everyone from Buzz Lightyear to Humphrey Bogart and
Fred Flintstone to Arnold Schwarzenegger. If you want to play
the game and guess the movies, click the caption button at the
bottom right of the screen to hide or reveal the titles.

http://y2u.be/wPcapo5ZB_o

SIR DOSSER, DJANGO AND THE ACTRESS

Legendary Mila Kunis interview with rookie reporter

It was BBC reporter Chris Stark's big break – an interview with Hollywood star Mila Kunis. The actress was meant to be promoting her new movie, *Oz the Great and Powerful*, but a mixture of bravado, nerves and a star clearly keen to take him off-piste led to the most down-to-earth interview ever. From his opening question – "Did you enjoy being ugly for once? Because, generally, like, you know, you're hot" – to asking her to be his plus-one at his mate Dicko's wedding, the whole thing is funny, charming and has given both their careers a deserved boost.

http://y2u.be/z4Ezruu1oeQ

BOO!

How to scare your boss – and keep your job

Ah! The simple ones are the best. An empty box and a big scream is all you need. We're watching an empty booze warehouse as one guy quietly goes about his work, "Bohemian Rhapsody" playing on the radio in the background. But what happened next caused this clip to be voted best video of the year on Jimmy Kimmel's hit US show. Look for the face pulled by Paul, the boss – that was the clincher for them. Just a word of warning for younger viewers, though: not all bosses are such good sports, so best leave the pranks to the professionals.

http://y2u.be/Uu80TPja2OY

APOCALYPSE AAAAAAAAAAHH!

The job interview at the end of the world

It's a job interview and you know you should be giving your prospective boss your full attention, but you spot something out of the corner of your eye that distracts you, someone rummaging through the drawers in the corner perhaps, a strange photograph or maybe a stray nostril hair. But what if the distraction was the actual end of the world? At what point do you draw your interviewer's attention to this? That's the premise for this well-enacted prank set up by LG to show off its high-definition TV screens.

http://y2u.be/Cer8I4cX-vs

YOUR NEW BEST FRIEND

The ultimate dog tease

Is Andrew Grantham a cruel heartless monster whose idea of fun is to drive his poor dog Clyde to distraction? After all, in separate videos – this one and *Dog Wants a Kitty* – we find him repeatedly goading Clyde into a frenzy of expectation before pitilessly letting him down. The answer is no, Andrew is actually a clever Canadian voiceover comedian whose talking-dog videos are brilliantly timed, expertly voiced and, it has to be said, perfectly acted by Clyde. These videos certainly reach out to a certain audience. They each have millions of hits – and only a thousand or so are mine.

http://y2u.be/nGeKSiCQkPw

LITTLE DRUMMER BOY

Time to wake the backseat drummer

It's great when your toddler falls asleep in the car. You get a rare minute to yourself or a chance to chat to your partner without an interruption every 20 seconds. But there is also a downside. When the kid wakes up, he or she is almost always whiney, grumpy and cranky. But these parents have found the perfect solution to that waking problem. Yep, they start blasting Nirvana's "Breed" from the car stereo and, before he's even opened his eyes properly, the little rocker is air drumming like some sad 20-something stoner. Magic.

http://y2u.be/oRm8RmNGFq4

ANTARCTIC ROLL

Penguins doing what they do best – falling over!

They call these guys "nature's comedians". The Antarctic might be cold but it must be one hell of a place for laughs with so many penguins shuffling around. We may not be able to get into their stand-up comedy clubs or laugh along with their sitcoms, but we do get to watch the little fellas falling over, again and again. And you can't deny they make you laugh – their miniature evening dress colouring, that cute little waddle and the unfortunate fact that these unstable creatures have to walk around on ice. Move over, Monty Python!

http://y2u.be/Tcx6YyXvvRI

SOCKS ROCKS!

Shetland pony dances his way to fame

Phone network Three are pretty keen on their online ads and had a 2014 hit with "Sing it Kitty" (the girl riding on the bike with a kitten in the basket). But Socks, the moonwalking Shetland pony, captured everyone's hearts in their most successful effort. Socks' dance track of choice was Fleetwood Mac's "Everywhere", but it was the blond-maned pony's nifty hoofwork that really caught the eye. He even made a comeback, wearing a Christmas sweater, for a festive campaign. Quite what it had to do with a mobile phone was anyone's guess but, frankly, who cares?

http://y2u.be/Ekr05T9Iaio

TURNING ON THE TAP

"Cups" – the hit tap-dancing version

Tap dancing? Isn't that only done by eight-year-old girls? Hasn't it gone the way of telephone boxes, ventriloquists and sets of *Encyclopaedia Britannica*? Well, no, apparently not, as it's alive and kicking, and these guys are the ones making sure tap dancing is trending. Anna Kendrick's massive hit "Cups (When I'm Gone)" inspired countless YouTube covers, but Christopher Rice and his fellow Broadway dancers clacking and clicking their way through the song is head, shoulders, knees and toes above them all – skilful, subtle, elegant, energetic and, well, pretty damn cool.

http://y2u.be/Q4FYNF02yEM

HITCH-A-RIDE HERO

Just about the strangest news report ever

This clip comes from a local TV news channel in Fresno, California, and tells how a man claiming to be Jesus drove his car into a roadside worker and then attacked a female bystander. So far, so newsworthy. But wait. A homeless hitchhiker, who had also been in the car, turned out to be the hero of the hour, saving the woman by attacking the driver with a small axe he happened to be carrying(!). Now, you must admit, it's getting strange, but that's not the half of it. Wait until you hear Kai the Hitchhiker retell the story (with adult language). Mind-blowing!

http://y2u.be/-Xa0NfCdLk4

GRANNY THEFT AUTO

Underage joyrider

"No videos games for an entire weekend." That's what Latarian Milton, a boy from South Florida, thinks his punishment should be for totalling his granny's car. Milton and his buddy wanted to do "hood-rat stuff" (as you do), so he took his grandma's Dodge Durango for a ride around the neighbourhood. He hit a couple of cars in a car park and managed to write off the SUV, but what really caught the police's attention was that he couldn't see over the steering wheel. Latarian, you see, is only seven years old!

http://y2u.be/qcqOgnQyXp4

BOXING CLEVER

How much fun can a cat have with a box?

It seems the answer is hours and hours of boundless enjoyment.
For us the question is: how long can we watch a cat having fun
with a box? If this video is anything to go by, it's pretty easy to fill
a good 90 seconds. For this is Maru, a 5.5kg (12lb) Scottish Fold
from Japan, who is fast becoming the Internet's favourite feline.
Maru's working hard for the fame as he has now appeared
in around 200 YouTube videos, mainly jumping in and out of
boxes, but, hey, if you've got a talent, why not milk it?

http://y2u.be/hPzNI6NKAG0

BRING HOME THE BACON

The remarkable Illinois state fair hog-calling contest

This is brilliant. And possibly useful. Because you never know when you might need to know exactly how to call a pig. He could be right over the other side of the field and he's not going to come if you just stand around shouting, "Hey, fatso, come over here." Oh no. These are professional callers with any number of tricks up their snouts, so sit back and prepare to go hog-wild for a hilarious feast of screams, shouts, whines, guttural emissions, snorts and a surprising number of "Here Piggy, Piggy!" calls.

http://y2u.be/uVcVSEa_Ooo

SHOUT AND FALL

Blink and you'll miss it

This one is for all those with short attention spans. Still with us? OK. See if you can hang in there till the end, although it does last a whole three seconds, so best bring a snack and a drink to keep you going. It's worth staying with it, though, because it could be the funniest three seconds on the net. And, of course, if you are the kind of person who can't stop laughing at someone falling over, some kind soul has compiled a feature length version in *Go Bwah 10 Minute Repeat*.

http://y2u.be/MXgnIP4rMol

MARTIAL ART FAIL

That'll be the universally feared, falling painfully move, then

---

Mark Hicks is a highly trained martial artist, stuntman and actor.
In one of YouTube's most famous clips, this video shows his
audition for a LeBron James Nike commercial. Hicks prepares to
perform his well-practised routine involving a back flip followed
by a display of his nunchuck skills. The cameras begin to roll.
Play video... hang on, you'll probably need to see that again —
and again. A great postscript is that, despite the epic fail
being leaked to YouTube, Mark was given another chance
to demonstrate his skills and actually got the part.

http://y2u.be/BEtloGQxqQs

OH, THE HUGE MANATEE!

When you just can't stop...

Why don't we see more manatees on our screens? These sea cows are calming, mesmerizing and have adorable, funny faces. Just because they don't enjoy savaging other creatures in bloodthirsty attacks, they hardly ever get an up-close documentary on the Discovery Channel. One of them did, however, get a breakthrough viral appearance in a clip that is guaranteed to raise a smile. So, full marks to producer Jordan Mencel for masterfully using Flux Pavilion's massive hit "I Can't Stop" as the perfect soundtrack and transforming an amusing 10-second film into a now legendary YouTube gem.

http://y2u.be/CLGJ-LVCQrM

ARMED ROBBERY RAP

One day all news interviews will be in song

Songify is a simple app that can turn speech into song. It's cheap and easy, so everybody's doing it, but it takes genius to do it with flair. Step forward the Gregory Brothers (under the YouTube username schmoyoho). The original footage was amusing enough – a slightly eccentric eye-witness account of an attempted armed robbery at a petrol station – but put to song it knocks most composed hits into a swag bag. And the lyrics are pretty smart too: "Cos my daddy taught me good" could have come from the lips of Beyoncé.

http://y2u.be/qloG4PlEPtY

FOOD FOR THOUGHT

Help yourself to a bowl of *Western Spaghetti*

Mmm! A delicious bowl of spaghetti with tomato sauce. You'll be licking your lips at the sight of this dish prepared by talented stop-motion artist Pes. But don't kid yourself you'll be able to re-create it at home. This is a cookery demonstration with a difference, as our chef makes use of the most incredible ingredients, including Rubik's Cube garlic, pick-up sticks spaghetti, Post-it note butter. And just wait to see what he uses for pepper. It's a feast for the imagination, if not exactly the stomach, and if this leaves you hungry for more, order up some of Pes' Oscar-nominated *Fresh Guacamole*.

http://y2u.be/qBjLW5_dGAM

ICE CREAM, YOU SCREAM

We all scream for coneing

Ing-ing is a popular pastime on YouTube. We've had planking (lying down), owling (perching) and batmanning (hanging upside down), but it's quite a feat to make up your own "ing" and see it take off across the net. Australian Albi Stevens managed just that. Albi's fast food videos are loved by millions as he befuddles, infuriates and occasionally amuses fast food drive-thru attendants with his pranks. But it is his coneing – grabbing the ice cream by the soft cream and not the cone – that really took off. Even Justin Bieber has posted his own cone-ing video!

http://y2u.be/nn1vMhsePOg

DESTRUCTION CYCLE

Hang on – I've left a sock in there

Russian anarchist Mikhail Bakunin wrote, "The lust of destruction is also a creative lust." He'd have loved this video, if he hadn't been dead for nearly 150 years. After all, at some level, we all like smashing something up for the sheer fun of it (don't you?) and Aussie50, producer of this epic five minutes, certainly does. Having taken out the concrete counterweight and put a few hefty objects in for a good wash, Aussie50 then selects what he refers to as the "kill cycle". What happens next is pretty impressive. Just don't try it with your mum's new Zanussi.

http://y2u.be/6_PLnInsh7E

SKIP TO THE GOOD BIT

Skipping – from the rope's point of view

You probably realize by now that YouTube is not the only video-sharing website in town; Vimeo, Vine and others increasingly have their own fans. However, if there's anything excellent posted on one of them, it will likely pop up on the others. Take this fantastic video from Callum Cooper. A fashion film for clothing company Klezinski, it was originally posted on Vimeo. Hypnotic, mesmerizing, beautifully filmed (if slightly nausea-inducing in a rollercoaster kind of way), it takes a unique perspective on a gentle rope-jumping game. Fabulously edited with a great soundtrack, it'll leave you in a spin.

http://y2u.be/x1G2QrasPRk

GIANT GUITARS OR SMALL CHILDREN?

Bizarre footage of North Korean child guitarists

North Korea is one of the world's most secretive states. Very little escapes across its closed borders, but this video was somehow smuggled out. What does it reveal about the North Koreans? That they are unable to manufacture child-sized guitars? That their hairdressing skills lag behind those of the West? Or that they're ready to invade the rest of the world if we ever unleash Jedward upon them? "Creepy as hell" reads the subtitle for the video. That's as maybe, but these kids can't half play a mean guitar!

http://y2u.be/gSedE5sU3uc

GAME OVER

Shooting from the hipster of YouTube

This one is for the dudes who like games such as *Halo* or *Call of Duty* – adventures played out through the eyes of the gamer. Although these games are, of course, incredibly realistic, filmmaker and visual-effects wizard Freddie Wong has taken it one big step further. Freddie is a YouTube legend with many viral gaming-based hits under his belt, but this is his most popular effort yet – a kind of scary, kind of funny, vision of a future game in which reality and fantasy are totally blurred.

http://y2u.be/CyCyzBOCedM

EXTRACTION DISTRACTION

Now we know why they're called wisdom teeth

Having your wisdom teeth out – a painful experience for some but a goldmine for those wanting entertaining videos. Pulling fabulous faces with their swollen cheeks, trying to communicate though still groggy from the anaesthetic and seemingly living in a strange parallel world, these post dental-trauma sufferers are earnest and befuddled – and a real hoot. Just watch Julie as she struggles with issues of time travel and tries to solve the case of the missing hat. And when the laughing gas starts to wear off, try *I'm a Nascar Driver* or *Unicorn After Wisdom Teeth*.

http://y2u.be/zgB2ziyAtel

THE WORLD AT HIS FEET

Remarkable footage of five-year-old Lionel Messi

Remember that boy who could run rings around everyone at playtime football? He was the star of the school team and was even invited to the local club for trials. He's now working in the estate agents in the high street nursing a dodgy knee. But for the little lad slipping through the toddler opposition in this film, the future panned out just the way it looked like it would because, 20 years later, Lionel Messi would be the best footballer in the world.

http://y2u.be/Dc8azekvE_s

YOU TALKIN' 'BOUT ME?

The name is the game in a hilarious conference prank

Now it's time for some good, old-fashioned, juvenile fun. There are always some laughs to be had at those big conventions where everyone is forced to wear a name badge, and American comedian Jack Vale totally nails it at the National Association of Music Merchants (NAMM) conference. He's got a good plan and he executes it well, so it's a sure-fire winner. After all, what would you do if you walked past a complete stranger who's talking about you on the phone? Gratifyingly simple and gloriously silly.

http://y2u.be/6w3QmqqCmk0

THE CAT THAT GOT THE CREAM

The Internet phenomenon that is Simon's Cat

You've probably come across Simon's Cat already, maybe in a book or a newspaper cartoon strip, but if you haven't seen his YouTube films, you're in for a real treat. Creator Simon Tofield's very short, simple, but quirky animations of his mischievous, but endearing, mog (actually based on all three of his own cats) all garner millions of views. There are nearly 50 videos featuring the adventures of the ever-hungry cat. *Let Me In* is a classic episode, which will have you scratching at the door desperate for more.

http://y2u.be/EKvNqe8cKU4

CRASH COURSE

Tribute to the daddy of the monster trucks

Monster trucks are five tons of big, big, noisy fun. OK, they're in real races, but what the punters want to see is these behemoths smashing and crashing their way around a circuit. The Grave Digger is the Godzilla of them – a green-and-black car crusher with menacing red headlights, it never disappoints. With a blatant disregard for the rules of the road and safety in general (do they even have wing mirrors?), these poster boys of the monster-truck world indulge in wild stunts and rollover crashes, and still win the race!

http://y2u.be/WwjGo3kQgMw

ON HIS TROLLEY

Taking a luxury ride

Next time you visit your local supermarket and wonder what's
happened to all the trolleys, here's your answer. The local pooches
are using them as mobility carts. Watch here as Maymo, the
lemon beagle, pushes his puppy sister Penny through the town
to the playground. All very cute, but it raises some serious
questions. Where would a dog get the token or coin to release the
trolley in the first place? Couldn't they do something more
useful, like get the weekly shopping? And who is carrying
the little plastic bags for their "gifts"?

http://y2u.be/cVg2QEYtdlM

DON'T LOSE YOUR HEAD

The wonderful world of exploding princesses

Simone Rovellini is a bit of a scamp. A digital artist, he excels in "doctoring" well-known films for comic effect. To be honest, Simone is a bit of a one-trick pony, but hey, it's a pretty good trick – he makes your favourite characters' heads explode! His morbidly hilarious video *Exploding Actresses* saw the likes of Julie Andrews, Judy Garland and Ingrid Bergman get the treatment. They were all fair game but this time he's surely taken it too far. Snow White? Cinderella? The Little Exploding Mermaid? Come on, Simone, have a heart!

http://y2u.be/i6cb0ggl8bQ

CHRISTMAS RAPPING

Sick bucket ready – it's a family Christmas video

We've all received those sickeningly smug Christmas cards that, rather than simply saying "Happy Holidays", proceed to fill you in on everything the family has done over the year, from little Archie learning to ride a bike to Mum burning the cupcakes. Well, things have just got worse – people have started to do video versions.

To be fair, the Holderness family's effort is as smart as their Christmas pyjamas as they rap about everything from four-year-old Penn Charles' school recital to six-year-old Lola's ability to count to 100 in Chinese... to Dad's recent vasectomy.

http://y2u.be/2kjoUjOHjPl

A REAL CRY BABY

A mother's song is all too emotional

This 10-month-old's response to her mother's performance of Rod Stewart's "My Heart Can't Tell You No" has brought tears to the eyes of thousands of YouTube viewers. If you want to see the strength of the bond between a mother and her child, just watch baby Mary-Ann's face as she listens to the delightful recital. The way she experiences the emotion of the song is incredibly moving and, as the tears well up in her eyes... hold on there, can someone pass me a tissue...

http://y2u.be/nIsCs9_-LP8

UNDERCOVER VIRTUOSO

World famous musician takes to the subway

Here's a question for you: if Beyoncé was singing on a street corner, how long would it take for her to draw a crowd? If Justin Bieber set about busking, how quickly would he fill his cap with loose change. Pretty quickly, yeah? So how about if one of the world's most famous musicians began to play at a busy rail station? The *Washington Post* set up an experiment to find out, persuading violin virtuoso Joshua Bell to flex his much-revered elbow at a Washington DC subway station. What happened next? Take a look...

http://y2u.be/hnOPu0_YWhw

BEDTIME FOR YAUN ZAI

Panda mum deals with the universal parenting problem

In the panda enclosure at Taiwan's Taipei Zoo, Yuan Yuan
is trying to get her youngster Yuan Zai to sleep.
"Come on now, bedtime."
"Oh Mum! Just 10 more minutes? Please."
"Bed!"
"Can I have a drink of water?"
"Nope. You're coming with me."
"Mum, I'm not even tired."
"When I say bed, I mean bed. You need your sleep.
Just look at those rings around your eyes!"

http://y2u.be/eRP3h2Lt6wQ

WHAT WERE YOU THINKING?

Barista sends girl his best "seduction" video message

Brody Ryan really thought he was in with a chance. This gorgeous girl had given the barista her number after they'd met at Starbucks. So, in a bid to impress, our wannabe Don Juan sent her a 16-second clip of himself with Drake's "Hold On We're Going Home" playing in the background... uh-oh. She passes the video to a friend who posts it online. Within days, there are hundreds of views and, in no time at all, the *Starbucks Drake Hands* parodies begin... and from Gremlins to Toddlers to Boston Terriers, they're all pretty good.

http://y2u.be/4ki-5_BD7ZwThe

THE DOMINO EFFECT

The greatest falling domino chain ever

If you've ever tried to set up one of those falling-domino chains, you'll know just how difficult it is. You spend ages placing them in exactly the right position and the dog walks over them or you sit back, admire your handiwork, topple the first domino, watch six more fall and then the whole thing comes to a frustrating halt. So, little surprise that it took three months for Hevesh5 and Millionendollarboy to set up more than 20,000 dominoes for these amazing tricks – and just minutes to knock them all down.

http://y2u.be/ARM42-eorzE

KILL BILL BABY

Soft toy no match for infant assassin

This thrilling trailer, an homage to both Quentin Tarantino's *Kill Bill* series and *Enter the Dragon*, features the latest in martial-art stars, Romeo Elvis Bulte Boivin. He's got the Bruce Lee moves, the Chuck Norris toughness, the Jackie Chan suppleness and he's a cute as a button — because Romeo is only a year old. So when a plushie dragon enters the arena (or back garden, as it is here), he's definitely no match for the soft-toy killer, who is all set to knock the stuffing out of him — quite literally.

http://y2u.be/1oHWvFrpocY

WATCH MY LIPS!

What the trombone saw...

And now for something completely different... David Finlayson, the second trombonist in the New York Philharmonic, decided to record an instrument's-eye view of his performance by attaching a camera to his trombone slide. The result is probably quite interesting to musicians and academics, but definitely very amusing to the rest of us. And, if not for his recital, Mr Finlayson certainly deserves a standing ovation for refusing to carry irritating ads on his clip, despite the opportunity to make a few bucks from his most entertaining experiment. Bravo David, bravo!

http://y2u.be/soDn2puEuL8

PUPPET SHOW AND TELL

When kids' TV goes feral

Freaky, freaky, freaky. Is this an attempt at a children's-TV puppet show or something much darker? What begins as a friendly educational guide to creativity seems to turn into something very different. It's led to a fair amount of Internet discussion on the meaning of the video — often centring on how children are conditioned to think in certain ways by patronizing TV and videos like these. Both amusing and unsettling, it's a fascinating piece. And maybe you can work out just why green isn't a creative colour.

http://y2u.be/9C_HReR_McQ

BATHTIME FOR KITTY

Cats and the wet stuff – what's not to like?

Just who is the most popular YouTube personality? Bieber, PSY, Miley? Maybe, but they all look jealously at the view count racked up by the domestic cat. Yep, kitty steals the show every time. This video explores that love/hate (OK, mostly hate) relationship between cats and water. Baths, sinks, taps, rivers and swimming pools – they do seem to bring out the playful, the weird, the cute and the downright funny in our furry friends. So by the time you read this, this video will have clocked up around 100 million views – Miley's got to go some to match that!

http://y2u.be/jQZtk-fCWQ4

LIKE SCIENCE CLASS – BUT FUN

Put a little Vsauce on your web

Michael Stevens' Vsauce channel almost single-handedly prevents YouTube being classed as a moronic collection of people falling over, showing off or appearing in dubious music videos. Vsauce is a collection of bite-sized videos that reflect a "hyper-curiosity about the world". The short films on science, technology, nature and much more are arranged in various segments, including Mindblow (inventions), FAK (facts and knowledge trivia) and WAC (weird awesome crazy activities from around the world). Charming, engaging and amusing, Stevens is like your favourite-ever science teacher and his lessons only ever last around five minutes!

http://y2u.be/jHbyQ_AQP8c

THE TIPPING POINT

A $200 tip – that must be some service!

How much do you tip for really good service at your local restaurant? 10 percent? Maybe 15 percent if you're in a good mood or even 20 percent if the waiter or waitress is cute. They get a small bonus to the measly wage they are paid and you get a nice smile and leave feeling like you are a pretty decent stand-up guy. But this crowd decided to take the whole tipping scenario even further. They decided to leave $200 tips for waiting staff earning not much more than $2 an hour – then film their reactions. Perhaps it's no surprise to discover they are pretty pleased...

http://y2u.be/Q4enUE8qt_Q

ELASTIC MAN

Stretchiest skin world record demonstration

The *Guinness World Records* annals are always worth peeking into for entertaining freaks. Here, Garry Turner, who's able to pull the skin of his stomach out nearly 16cm (6¼in), shows what he's made of. Some skill, you may think. He must have worked hard at that. However, to Garry, it all comes easily. He suffers from a rare medical condition called Ehlers-Danlos Syndrome. Just think — once upon a time, you had to go to a circus to be freaked out. Now you can squirm at the touch of a button.

http://y2u.be/f46SpiboAew

GANDALF ON ACID

Classic old-man-invades-interview clip

It's one of the iconic YouTube videos. This 30-second clip in which an old bloke encroaches on a TV interview has been viewed by millions of people. And you can bet most of them had at least a little chuckle. The ol' fella from the city of Rethymnon, Crete, who has been nicknamed "Greek Grandpa" and "Gandalf on Acid", put in one of the great comedy performances of our time and was rewarded with his own five minutes of fame.

http://y2u.be/iheOMq8UkN4

CUTEST DOG ON THE PLANET

Meet Boo the dog – he's too cute!

"My name is Boo. I am a dog. Life is good" is how this Pomeranian launched his journey to fame. He is now an Internet sensation with 10 million Facebook "likes", his own publications, a job as Virgin America's "spokesdog" and an endorsement by Khloe Kardashian, who says he is, indeed, the "cutest dog on the planet". So here's your chance to see what all the fuss is about. Boo being shy, Boo dressed up, Boo playing with a soft toy. It's nothing any old mongrel hound couldn't do, but there's no denying it: this dog is darned cute.

http://y2u.be/peKSCssJTqE

FLIPPING BRILLIANT!

Cristiano Ronaldo comes to life in a flipbook

Etoilec1 is a bit of a mystery figure. No one seems to know much about him, except he can certainly draw! He has done some impressive manga-type flip books and a great "Gangnam Style" book, but he is really inspired when it comes to drawing footballers. He's paid flip-book homage to Ronaldinho, Zlatan Ibrahimovic and Lionel Messi, but it's the extravagant skills of the Portuguese prodigy Cristiano Ronaldo that really come to life on his pages. And not a theatric tumble in sight!

http://y2u.be/-DGs-ZQMqhg

TRAFFIC JAM

White Van Man sings the blues

White Van Man has a bad reputation. The drivers and passengers of these utility vehicles are often seen as sexist, angry and belligerent. These two guys might have been actors paid by the White Van Man publicity department to improve their image. But they're not. They're just two working blokes on the way to a job, having a laugh as their favourite tune blasts from the van's speakers. It's a hoot!

http://y2u.be/urPq6PVa3-o

YOUTUBE BY POST

Enjoy YouTube offline

Spare a thought for those people who find the Internet daunting and unreliable. How do you find what you want? How do you know someone's not watching you through your computer or tablet? And where do all these videos come from? In 2012 those thoughtful people at YouTube took note of these concerns and announced this amazing service – all of YouTube on DVD delivered to your door! No more worries about download capacity or streaming capabilities. Just pop a disk into your player.
Note: this video was posted on 1 April...

http://y2u.be/Y_UmWdcTrrc

SMALL GIRL, BIG BIRD, PONY

An epic encounter

Here's a nice little clip of a small girl taking her first ride on
her pony. She trots around in a field quite happily, but then a
long-legged bird monster appears and things go all Pete
Tong – in the most hilarious way. So who will win? The pony
and the toddler or the adult ostrich? Who's your money on?
Do keep watching to the end, though. The pony does
a fabulous "nothing to do with me" exit.

http://y2u.be/AlO0x2gAnvM

SILENT ERA CELL PHONE

Time traveller spotted in Charlie Chaplin film

People today, eh? They can't do anything without taking their phone along and yapping continuously. You'd think if you managed to time travel back to the 1920s, you'd have something better to do than call your friend to discuss who said what to whom. But consider this bystander found on the extras on the DVD of Charlie Chaplin's 1928 film *The Circus.* She really does seem to be chatting on her phone. Explain that one, then!

http://y2u.be/TilrpEMbQ2M

DUNKIN' DOBBIN

Horse tries out new jumping technique

Compared with humans, animals always manage to look so graceful and co-ordinated. You never see them walking into lampposts, tripping over their own feet or taking the stairs seven at a time. Take the horse, for example – serene when still, graceful at a trot and powerful at full speed. You would never get a thoroughbred making a complete ass of himself, would you? Well, somehow this nag manages to prove the exception. Memorize his face and remember not to back him in a steeplechase.

http://y2u.be/YBkmefIlgiE

DEMON DOG

Staines gets psyched by cupcakes

Anyone who's seen the iconic *Dramatic Chipmunk* YouTube clip will know where this one is heading. It features Staines, an Australian Shepherd dog, who is appearing on a TV dog-training show. For the discipline test, the dog is presented with a plateful of cupcakes and must retain its self-control. As the strain begins to show, it seems that the only way Staines will get through it is to enter a zen-like trance...

http://y2u.be/t-XIMEHGoZI

DAD DENIAL DANCE

Andrew and his famous "not the father" moves

You may have seen this in the background of the hit movie
Bridesmaids, but it's worth a giggle or two in its own right. This
is a segment from US TV's *The Maury Povich Show* on US TV,
where private domestic disputes are aired in public. Now, for
many men, the moment they discover they're a father is one they
treasure for life. But not Andrew. He's been told by the child's
mother that she's 5,000 percent sure she's had his baby,
but he's holding out for the DNA test to prove otherwise.
Will he be proud as punch or quietly relieved? Oh no...

http://y2u.be/vt2i0ts-uck

GONE WITH THE WIND

Hurricane "Bawbag" rolls into town

Mother Nature has a pretty good sense of humour at times. Here, she's whipped up a rare old storm in Cowdenbeath, Scotland, with gusts reaching up to 265km/h (165mph). Although such winds are often destructive, ruining people's houses and lives, in this particular case old Mrs N has just decided to have a laugh. Fortunately, local resident Conor Guichan was filming the hurricane through his window at the time – and manages to provide the perfect commentary as an unusual object sweeps past his window...

http://y2u.be/UPKb9z4I7eM

MASHED UP WITH KETCHUP

Ketchup robot with epic soundtrack

Looking for a good-value video? Then check this out: two
YouTube classics for the price of one. Firstly, you get to watch
the almost amazing *Ketchupbot*. Actually called the Automata,
it's an invention straight from the world of Wallace and Gromit,
because a robot ketchup dispenser would be absolutely awesome
if, well, it worked. But never fear, for the soundtrack is YouTube's
infamous *20th Century Fox Fanfare Played on Flute* (in fact,
a recorder), a travesty so perfectly executed that it
fits the video like a glove.

http://y2u.be/4WX58CZwyiU

MARRY ME, LIVE

After this, the wedding had better be good...

OK, you'll either love this or really hate it. Perhaps the latter if you don't consider it romantic to share your marriage proposal with anyone who has an Internet connection or if your idea of spontaneity doesn't involve roping in every long-lost relation, friend and passing acquaintance and spending hours in rehearsal. However, the resulting video has been enjoyed by over 25 million viewers and even the most cynical of us might have to admit to a lump in the throat when Isaac finally pops the question. It would be even funnier if she said "no", though!

http://y2u.be/5_v7QrlW0zY

KING OF THE SWINGERS

It's the largest rope swing in the world!

When these guys built a rope swing, they didn't just chuck a rope
over the nearest branch. They made the largest rope swing in
the world. Their carefully constructed rig was built over a natural
sandstone structure called Corona Arch in Moab, Utah, USA. It
had a pendulum 75m (250ft) long and a drop of 45m (150ft)
before the rope even got taut. But this was no child's play. If
the set-up went wrong, there would be serious consequences.
After it went viral, adrenaline-fuelled daredevils flocked
to ride the arch, until a tragic accident led to the
authorities drastically restricting its use.

http://y2u.be/4B36Lr0Unp4

KITTY GRINDING THE CRACK

Introducing the world's first BASE jumping cat

If you've watched the BASE jumper Jeb Corliss video *Grinding the Crack*, you will understand the joke here – it's even cut to the same music. If YouTube has done anything, it has proved that cats aren't always cool, they don't always land on their feet and they are as capable as looking as clumsy as a drunk in a supermarket. This cat does its utmost to be catlike. Inscrutable and thoughtful, it clearly has a plan, but it's not going to be rushed into action. Watch as it sizes up the situation, assesses the task and only then does it jump...

http://y2u.be/Veg63B8ofnQ

COMPLETELY BARKING

Weird dog with an even weirder bark

This is the dog's chops – a fantastic gabbling poodle-cross that sounds as weird as it looks. You might be tempted to wonder just what it's talking about, but I really wouldn't bother. If you did manage to translate the strange yelpings, they'd probably be the equivalent of that strange bloke at the bus stop screaming, "The cucumbers are coming to get us. Guard your rawlplugs!" But if you enjoy this – and you will – be sure to check out *Videoresponse to The Weirdest Dog Ever*, then explain what that's all about!

http://y2u.be/IvD8WcrdK5o

RETURN OF THE SINGING SPACEMAN

Space station star Chris Hadfield is back on the radar

Chris Hadfield's amazing film of his cover of David Bowie's "Space Oddity" recorded at the International Space Station was one of the most talked about YouTube videos ever. But there's more to the commander than a good voice. In fact, he's made a fascinating array of videos of life in space, from *How to Wash Your Hand in Space* to *How to Make a Sandwich in Space*. But the Canadian astronaut has also furthered his recording career with ISS (Is Someone Singing/International Space Station), a duet in which Chris performs his part in space, while Barenaked Ladies' frontman Ed Robertson sings along in downtown Toronto.

http://y2u.be/AvAnfi8WpVE

A SELFIE-MADE MAN

The selfie is dead. Long live the super-selfie!

It all happened a couple of years ago. Suddenly, everyone was taking a selfie – a picture of themselves that said, "Look at me! Aren't I just the most fun guy ever?" When President Obama was seen taking a selfie at Nelson Mandela's funeral it seemed the whole world had gone mad. But wait. Gabriel Valenciano was working on a super-selfie – a series of pictures in which the hyperactive 1980s gym throwback works it to the *Space Jam* soundtrack. In 15 top YouTube seconds, he smashes it with excess energy, enthusiasm and humour. Top effort.

http://y2u.be/Sp9xfM6SSTI

COOL CROW

A brilliant bird who likes to hit the slopes

If you thought snowboarding 10-year-olds speeding past you
on the slopes was humiliating enough, wait until you see this
common garden bird practicing on a board. It isn't actually a
bird-sized snowboard, but a lid from a mayonnaise jar,
but there's no doubting that he's using it to ride the snow
and going back for more. It's quite a recent clip so
expect more in the extreme-bird-sport series, maybe
a pigeon on a BMX or a seagull on a surfboard?

http://y2u.be/n7hiuXjXJEw

DANGEROUS DINNER DATE

More animals eating their food

MisterEpicMann and friends took the biscuit for Britain's YouTube video of the year for their imitations of the table manners of various animals. It may not be exactly educational but it certainly caught the imagination of the online community, who contributed many of their own tributes and parodies. Best leave it to the experts, though, so thankfully, the original creators have returned with part two, which includes a hawk, a cheetah, a fruit fly (disgusting!) and an octopus. Now, you may think it's just slapstick but, as you shake your head at the nonsense people watch, I bet you can't suppress a little chuckle here and there.

http://y2u.be/lp2qchPjk-l

HAMBURGER HERO

Cleveland kidnapping rescuer's meaty interview

"I barbeque with this dude. We eat ribs and whatnot!" In helping to save three women and a girl from dreadful captivity in a Cleveland cellar, Charles Ramsey became a national hero in the US. But in giving one of the best TV news interviews ever, the effusive 43-year-old became an Internet sensation. They should show this to all novice reporters as an example of how to add excitement, colour, product endorsement and a little fun to even the grimmest of stories – even if he did appear to stretch the facts at times!

http://y2u.be/gcLSl3oyqhs

PING-PONG PADDLE POW!

Awesome table tennis bat knife-flicking stunt

This is a version of ping-pong you won't have seen before. Out of Sweden came this 30-odd-second clip showing a guy using table tennis bats to propel knives that an accomplice catches with her own outstretched bats. Pretty amazing, but they then take the whole stunt to an even more extreme level. "Unbelievable!" you cry. And you have a point. Now take a look at the YouTube video *Miss Ping Debunk*. In a few witty and entertaining minutes, Captain Disillusion completely deconstructs the stunt, showing exactly how they faked the extraordinary trick.

http://y2u.be/5NO-fka_JTQ

WHO'S IN CHARGE?

Advice from the little backseat driver

YouTube is full of cute kids saying sweet or clever things, but this one does stand out. It features dad Ryan Hunley as he offers to help August, his young daughter, buckle herself into her car seat. Now, August has reached the independent old age of two and doesn't consider she needs her father's meddling anymore. Will she forgive him for posting it when she's older? Well, in a short interview on *"Have You Ever Had a Dream Like This" Kid – 14 Years Later*, the most famous YouTube child ever didn't seem to mind.

http://y2u.be/4A6Bu96ALOw

(NEAR) DEATH OF A SALESMAN

Racing driver takes a test drive like no other

As ads for soft drinks go, this is a super-fizzy prank. Jeff Gordon, the famous American racing-car driver, is disguised and "geeked up" before calling on a car dealer. Eager to secure a deal, the salesman encourages him to take a test drive in the speedy Chevy Camaro. However, once behind the wheel, our nervous nerd becomes a little too bold... and, if you wonder if the video is real, watch *Test Drive 2*, where Jeff plays another high-speed prank on a car journalist who doubted him in print.

http://y2u.be/f1sL-lto4sw

PET SOUNDS

Time for a little cat chat

Talking cats, eh? So what do they talk about? Tales of last night's scrap with next-door's ginger tom? That annoying bloke who kicks them every time his girlfriend leaves the room? Or the science behind that whole length of whisker/width of body equation? If this video is anything to go by, YouTubers Talking Animals seem to have a pretty good idea of feline banter. These two kitties have a neat line in petty arguments and sneaky plans to get treats, all performed with extraordinary realism. Nine out of ten comments agree – it's a winner!

http://y2u.be/1JynBEX_kg8

HARRY POTTERFY'S THE WORLD

More magic from Potter Puppet Pals

It has now been over seven years since Neil Cicierega's magnificent, slightly off-message Harry Potter puppet series went on YouTube. The third episode, *The Mysterious Ticking Noise*, remains in the Top 50 most-viewed videos ever. The puppet characters are very loosely based on the popular series, but while JK Rowling's Harry Potter series has long since come to an end, Potter Puppet Pals continue to produce high-class episodes. This 2013 short – only 53 seconds long – sees the Pals' ever-vain and arrogant Harry finding a solution to everyone's problems, even the viewers'.

http://y2u.be/QM-TT6KTQNw

RED BULL WINGS

Adrenaline-fuelled mountain bike excitement

It's amazing. You can spend hour after hour, day after day, watching YouTube clips and you'll still come across something that completely blows you away. This is another video combining those old favourites – a GoPro camera and extreme sport – but this is possibly the best yet. New Zealand's Kelly McGarry is competing at the Red Bull Rampage, a notoriously gnarly downhill mountain-bike competition held in Utah, USA. The course itself is terrifying, but that's not enough for Kelly, who tops it by pulling off an incredible backflip over a 22m (72ft) canyon. He came second...

http://y2u.be/x76VEPXYaI0

FACE TO FACE

Reincarnation enacted in a trippy time-lapse self-portrait

This is the video artwork of British artist Emma Allen, whose self-portrait explores the idea of rebirth and illustrates the transfer of energy from one incarnation to another. In an incredible journey, the model's face is transformed through the ageing process until she resembles a white skull. It's mesmerizing to watch, but what happens next is totally surprising and beautiful. It took Emma five days of face painting and shooting to make all the frames for the animation, and she has been rewarded with a dreamlike 75 seconds that takes its place as a YouTube must-see.

http://y2u.be/07Ch4A9PnZI

DON'T LOSE YOUR MARBLES

The Internet sensation that is Jenna Marbles

According to the *New York Times*, Jenna Marbles is "the woman with one billion clicks". She is the most successful female poster on YouTube and 13 million YouTubers subscribe to her channel, where she offers advice on anything from *How To Trick People Into Thinking You're Good-Looking* to *A Drunk Make-Up Tutorial*. Jenna's operation is distinctly lo-fi – mostly shot in her own apartment using just a single fixed camera. She gets by because she is sassy, likeable and extremely funny. This is a pretty good example of her work, although she does tend to use fruitier language on many of her other videos.

http://y2u.be/dp-AxFdUe4A

MUTT WITH THE MOVES

Nathan, the happy dancing dog

Here's Nathan, whipping his hair back and forth and moving like he was born on the dance floor. Pharrell Williams' hit song "Happy" was everywhere in 2014 and was just crying out for someone to have a viral hit. So step forward, Nathan, possibly the ugliest dog in the world, for a well-earned five minutes of fame. And it couldn't be a lovelier story. Nathan was a rescue dog with quite a sad past but, by the look of things, he's settled down pretty well in his new home!

http://y2u.be/x_wgb1q1opQ

KUNG FU GRANDPA

Dead-beat commentary cuts
down nunchucking senior citizen

You know how it is: you head out early in the morning to an empty
supermarket car park to practise a few kung fu moves and give
your nunchucks a bit of air. Then, by the time you've got home
and sat down with a coffee, you discover you're the star
of a viral video and, to add insult... they're calling you
Kung Fu Grandpa. That's roughly what happened to 52-year-old
Tom Bell after a little workout in his local parking lot. And the
hilarious commentary? That's courtesy of one Rev. Aamon Miller,
a man of the cloth! Who can you trust? A real gem.

http://y2u.be/gYvw68IneV4

OFFICE CHAIR BOOGIE

The original *Numa Numa* guy

Gary Brolsma was one of the first YouTube stars and his *Numa Numa* video has now breached the 50-million-hit mark. The video is just a webcam recording of Gary sitting in his computer chair, infectiously lip-synching and dancing along to a 2003 song called "Dragostea din Tei" by Moldovan-Romanian boy band, O-Zone. This is YouTube at its best, spreading joy and a little magic,
so join those 50 million viewers and go watch it!

http://y2u.be/60og9gwKh1o

WHAT GOES UP...

Vertigo-inducing rock climbing madness

Skip this one if you're scared of heights, but the rest of you are
in for a treat, as rock climber Alex Honnold takes on El Sendero
Luminoso, a 457m (1,500ft) high wall in Mexico. Alex is a free
solo climber, meaning he goes up alone and he doesn't use ropes,
harnesses and other protective gear while climbing. There
is absolutely no room for error – even the slightest slip-up
would be catastrophic. If you can bear to watch to the hair-
raising end, you'll find a link to the full six-minute video.

http://y2u.be/wX_rh8Qugt0

BEHIND THE BRICKS

That hilarious *LEGO Movie* trailer

The blockbuster that was *The Lego Movie* probably didn't need a
lot of selling, but this featurette trailer is as good as marketing
can get. It works so well because, with tongues firmly in cheeks,
the characters, voiced by the actors, talk about the actors
playing them. Clever, eh? It's a complete hoot — and
where else do you get the chance to *actually* hear
Morgan Freeman read the telephone directory?

http://y2u.be/cH4tMSd3QJY

THE BOTTOM LINE

Miley's off to twerk

Miley Cyrus can hold her head up with pride. She was great in *Hannah Montana,* has a quadruple-platinum debut album, five non-consecutive Number One albums in the US and a fine collection of tattoos. But this is what she will be remembered for: a raunchy, and it has to be said cringe-making, performance alongside Robin Thicke at the VMA awards. The debate was instant – unacceptable behaviour or just a bit of fun? It became the most tweeted-about event in history and ensured even the furthest reaches of civilization now know how to "twerk".

http://y2u.be/YFLv9Ns1EuQ

IT WON'T TAKE A MINUTE

Sound advice in 59 seconds

Throw those diet books away. Here's 59 seconds of scientific
weight-loss advice. Psychologist Richard Wiseman, a former
magician with a PhD in the psychology of deception, has a
YouTube channel with over a million subscribers and 200 million
views. Prof Wiseman believes that tiny alterations in our lives can
make a huge difference to our overall happiness. His collection
of under-a-minute videos contain simple, science-based,
life-changing tips, from *How to Impress in Meetings* to
Cutting Down on Drinking the Easy Way and intriguing
bite-sized tests such as *Are You a Good Liar?*

http://y2u.be/zDGaXoMRLTU

THE SHINY GUY WORRIES

Star Wars explained by a three-year-old

If it's not bad enough that fully grown adults are attending *Star Wars* conventions in their droves and dressing up as star troopers or whatever, now they have resorted to forcing their children to explain the plot. Shouldn't there be laws about that kind of cruelty? To be fair, the cute kid in this famous clip does a pretty good job, nailing various characters, including C-3PO ("the shiny guy always worries") and Obi-Wan Kenobi ("he sometimes moves things around"). I know what you're thinking, though. Any chance of getting her to explain *The Matrix* trilogy?

http://y2u.be/EBM854BTGL0

UNHAPPILY EVER AFTER

The unfortunate fate of Disney princesses – in song

"And they all lived happy ever after." YouTuber Jon Cozart, aka Paint, takes the ending as the beginning in his Disney parody that went viral with 30 million views and counting. In a self-made, single-handed, barbershop quartet-style song, Paint takes four Disney princesses and explains what happened next. Mermaid Ariel is a victim of sea pollution; Jasmine's worried about Aladdin, who is locked up in Guantanamo; Pocahontas is a renegade killer; and Belle, well, she has a lot of explaining to do. It's witty, original and brilliantly executed – and Paint's *Harry Potter in 90 Seconds* is worth a quick look, too.

http://y2u.be/diU70KshcjA

TAKE A TABLET

Incredible iPad painting of Morgan Freeman

If you thought your iPad was useful only for playing Angry Birds
and catching up on *Game of Thrones* on your commute home,
have a look at what artist Kyle Lambert has been up to on his
tablet. Using only a finger, an iPad Air and the app Procreate,
we can watch a time-lapse record of his gobsmackingly realistic
portrait of actor Morgan Freeman. (It actually took him
200 hours and 285,000 brush strokes to complete.)
Of course, some claim it's a hoax but Kyle and the app
manufacturers are standing by the astonishing video.

http://y2u.be/uEdRLIqdgA4

WHO YOU LOOKING AT?

The ultimate showdown: animals vs mirrors

Doh! It's a mirror, stupid. Time to feel superior and watch cats, dogs, lizards and birds making fools of themselves in front of... themselves. Whether they're looking to impress, fight, mate or are just curious about their mirror image, they still end up looking pretty silly and, of course, kind of cute. The puppy backing off from its own image is particularly memorable. Yep, this confirms we humans really are the master species. Now let's go back to watching three hours of epic fails and people falling over...

http://y2u.be/FYm4RtBQncQ

PUPPY LOVE

Featuring the most patient cat in the world

Another day, another thousand cat videos appear on YouTube. But does anyone ever consider the workers? The poor moggies are forced to spend hours in rehearsals and make-up just to look extra cute in front of the camera, only to be rewarded with the odd treat or an old cotton reel... big deal.
The National Union of Cats is determined to put an end to the exploitation. Its members are hard-working and professional, and deserve more. Just look at the poise and patience of this kitty – he waited until the camera was turned off to savage the irritating pooch.

http://y2u.be/WHuaKpimSqg

TRICK IS THE TREAT

The fabulous return of the *Halloween Candy* prank

It's the gift that keeps on giving! For the third successive year, American TV-show host Jimmy Kimmel ran his *I Told My Kids I Ate All Their Halloween Candy Challenge* and was rewarded with another five minutes of angry, stomping, crying, howling brats – all distraught that their hard-earned sugar treats had been secretly pigged by their parents. Greedy and unforgiving children, heartless and cruel adults – it doesn't exactly show the human race in its best light, but it is utterly hilarious. And come on, admit it: you, too, half-regret the happy ending. If only the parents had actually eaten the sweets...

http://y2u.be/RK-oQfFToVg

OFF THE LINE

Best-ever goal line clearance

It's frustrating enough to see your goal-bound shot get cleared off the line, but when the opposition's last-gasp saviour isn't even one of their team you have a right to be annoyed. That's just what happens as Brazilian Série D club, Tuti, bear down on the goal of their opponents, Aparecidence. The defending team's masseur is the culprit/hero who keeps the game tied at 2–2 and sends Aparecidence through to the semi-finals. Quite whether the Tuti players have stopped chasing him yet hasn't been reported.

http://y2u.be/afhWQumYO24

DEAD GIVEAWAY MAGIC

Stuart shows he's got the Edge on other magicians

There's plenty of great magic on YouTube, but Stuart Edge's one dollar/thousand dollar-note trick has a feel-good factor many other contenders lack. Stuart (whose *Mistletoe Kissing Prank* is also quite sweet) selects those in need of a pick-me-up for his trick and allows them to keep whatever note magically appears in their hand. As you might imagine, the participants are genuinely bowled over.

http://y2u.be/7U1fuQF0KjQ

DUN-DUN, DUN-DUN, DUN-DUN, DUN-DUN

Sharks on film

Real-life shark footage can scare your pants off – those sleek movements, the naked aggression, those very pointy teeth – but you can also sit through hours of Discovery Channel or YouTube shark vids and find the moment of attack is all blurred by a mass of bubbles and a hastily departing diver. However, shark attacks in the movies deliver clear water, close-ups and acrobatic sharks with severed limbs in their mouths. Every detail is perfectly captured. This montage, put together by the *Huffington Post*, collects the best of big-screen attacks from *Jaws* to the *Deep Blue Sea*.

http://y2u.be/wnKrWOpUwR0

RUN RABBIT RUN

Sweary commentary on rabbit outrider

First, a warning: there's some pretty bad language bandied about on this video, so if that sort of thing offends, watch it on mute – it'll still make you smile. Now, do you remember that rabbit on the Duracell battery ad that kept running and running? Well, he's back – in real life! This is footage from railway engineer Craig Woods, featuring the voices of his pals, as their van tries to overtake a bunny on a Scottish country road. It's hilariously surreal.

http://y2u.be/wVN4PRLrpsA

BALL CONTROL

A sport that's bubbling under

Back when defenders were as hard as nails and forwards were nervous, football was a man's game. Nowadays, footballers are so pampered they might as well play in their own safe little bubbles. What? They already do? And it turns out to be very, very funny. The players are encased in zorb-like inflatable bubbles and are allowed to bounce into each other as they try to tackle. No one gets hurt and when they roll around like toy-town figures, trying to get back on their feet, it's highly entertaining. This has got to be the future of sport, hasn't it?

http://y2u.be/xll45f6i1PU

HEADBANGING FIREMAKING

Forget the Stone Age, welcome to the Rock Age

Don't worry. You're safe here. No actual rock music can be heard in this video. In fact, that's the real fun of it. All we hear is the soothing sounds of nature. If it wasn't for the Speedos, grungy shorts and T-shirts, this might pass for ancient footage of Neolithic man making fire while worshipping the great hair god. In these days of professional YouTubers, there's something reassuring about unintentionally funny footage still finding its way to a wide audience. This even has a perfect, almost poetic, ending. Rock on, dudes!

http://y2u.be/389DkzjHpus

PUCKER UP

20 strangers meet for a first kiss

It's a great idea: find 10 pairs of total strangers willing – after a short introduction and some small talk – to indulge in a "proper" first kiss. For all that this is an ad (for a clothing company) and the "strangers" are a little too relaxed and good-looking, it is sensitively observed (in black and white), charming and sensual. The kisses, some a little awkward, some more passionate, may call to mind your own first kiss. Or they might make you squirm and start shouting, "For heaven's sake – get a room!"

http://y2u.be/IpbDHxCV29A

MAN'S BEST FRIEND

If people were pets

This very funny film considers who makes for the better human companion – the over-affectionate hound or the indifferent mog? Fatawesome's unique spin is that they ask what life would be like if your mates acted like your pets. How would you cope with someone who greeted you like a long-lost friend when you'd only been out for five minutes? Or how would you feel about your buddy waking you up in the middle of the night because he fancied some cereal? They've also made an amusing sequel showing just how these pet "friends" can really mess up your life.

http://y2u.be/GbycvPwr1Wg

HEY PRESTO! AAAAAHHHH!

Magic trick with spectacular finale

Ah, the old tablecloth trick. Whipping a tablecloth from under a tea set without breaking your mum's best china can be pretty difficult to execute, but, as a magic trick, yawn! It's been done a million times and lacks any pizazz or excitement. However, these lads have got the tablecloth part down toa fine art and solved the problem by adding a finale that's surprising, dramatic and dangerous! Now all you have to work out is whether it's real or faked.

http://y2u.be/i8Nivk_0TkI

THEME PARK TORTURE

The rollercoaster ride he'll never forget

At most theme parks, they now film every single ride the punters take, so for a few notes, you and your friends can buy a souvenir. This is great, because when you get home, you can have a real laugh at your gurning and screaming faces in the minutes before your threw up behind the candy-floss stall. But there is a more sinister side to this practice. An employee is watching all those videos in the hope of finding a humiliating clip with which to blackmail some poor sap. Here's one who evidently never paid up – now, of course, a YouTube classic.

http://y2u.be/0MD6Cx0qzRA

GET YOU!

Singing policemen camp it up

One of the best moments of the Sochi Winter Olympics Games must have been the Russian Interior Ministry Police singing at the opening ceremony. While the London Olympics featured Paul McCartney, The Who and the Spice Girls, and Beyoncé appears at the opening of an envelope in the US, the Russians decided to humiliate their once-feared secret police by making them perform the campest rendition ever of Daft Punk's "Get Lucky". They make a pretty good fist of it but those interrogation rooms will never seem as intimidating again.

http://y2u.be/pOTt8QZWSdw

DESPOTIC DOODLES

North Korean dictator draws his life

Anyone who is anyone on YouTube is posting a "draw my life".
These are a series of stick drawings or scribbled figures on
a whiteboard that tell the events of a person's life. YouTube
celebs Jenna Marbles and Ryan Higa have both made funny and
poignant versions, but somehow Korean dictator Kim Jong-un has
got in on the act. His drawings tell of his remarkable birth, his
rise to fame, schooldays in "Sweetserland", losing weight and
his success with the ladies. YouTube is banned in North Korea,
but they have their own version of the Internet, where
this might well be repeated endlessly.

http://y2u.be/U_pZNH_ltDU

THE CALL OF THE WILD

Classic animal footage – with added soundtrack

Life in the wild can be a desperate bid for survival. Become too conspicuous and any minute could be your last. That's why animals communicate softly and without undue fuss. Just watch the subtle and understated way that this marmot attempts to contact his friend Alan – or could that be Steve? Meanwhile, in the depths of the ocean, the sharks practise their theme tune, knowing that one bum note could ruin the whole attack! There's plenty of voiced-over animal clips to choose from on YouTube, but this one combines two winners in a 90-second gem.

http://y2u.be/XgvR3y5JCXg

JUMPING TO CONCLUSIONS

Watch out for that bollard!

Parkour is so cool. It treats the urban environment as a natural obstacle course – the city becomes a physical challenge. To perform at the top level demands immense strength, amazing agility, bravery, a daredevil mentality and an up-to-date *A-Z*. Even the French name for the sport sounds cool. So it's extra fun when these ghetto gymnasts make real idiots of themselves in some of the most painful ways possible – and still try to maintain their dignity. We can reassure you that all of the participants in this hilarious video *were* harmed during the filming.

http://y2u.be/ZEs9zmF-Fwk

THE ONLY WAY IS ESSEX

Ellen DeGeneres' pint-sized protégées

YouTube has some extraordinary stories but few match the adventure of Sophia Grace Brownlee from Essex. In 2011, her aunt uploaded this video of Sophia Grace singing the Nicki Minaj rap "Super Bass" as her five-year-old cousin Rosie danced along. In two weeks, the video had gained over 40 million views. Soon, Sophia Grace and Rosie were being flown over to the USA to appear with Nicki on Ellen DeGeneres' hit TV show (you can see that on YouTube, too). Wowed by the girls' distinctive English accents and attitude, Ellen ensured they became the most popular (or irritating) English imports since Posh and Becks.

http://y2u.be/ti-IDMPIT_4

A DOGS' DINNER

Join Nono and Sia on a posh dinner date

"Hey, Sia, where are you having dinner tonight?"
"Same as ever – in the corner of the kitchen, right where they keep my bowl."
"Fancy something a little different?"
"Have you been stealing from the bin again, Nono?"
"No. I just thought we might go out."
"This isn't leading up to your Nandogs or McDogalds joke again, is it?"
"No, dawg! Get your best jumper on – we're going upmarket..."

http://y2u.be/EVwlMVYqMu4

MIND THE GAP, YAH

Posh boy Orlando becomes an intern

Posh student Orlando became an Internet celebrity after posting a series of videos of his calls to his friend Tarquin back in Fulham. Like many students, Orlando spent his gap year travelling the world in order to go on the lash and vomit over various third-world destinations. Orlando was too good a character for his creator Matt Lacey to lose so, now back from his "gap yah", we find him ringing to tell Tarquin all about his recent internships in "arrrt", the "meedjah" and "Parrr-liament".

http://y2u.be/hLm2wv4r2ss

MUTANT GIANT SPIDER DOG

Mayhem on the streets as the spider dog goes on the rampage

It looks real enough. And terrifying enough. A giant mutant spider is roaming the streets, chasing its victims into the enormous webs it has built. But this is the brilliant work of Polish YouTuber Sylwester Wardega. He has dressed his dog Chica in a spider costume, let him loose in the local streets, and filmed the ensuing mayhem. People going about their lives are naturally scared out of their wits and even more frightened as they come across the rope webs that Sylwester has rigged up, complete with fake human remains. His reward for such imagination was to earn the Number One "top trending video" of 2014.

http://y2u.be/YoB8t0B4jx4

ANACONDA DANCE TRIUMPH

**11-year-old dancer wins the internet
with her dance interpretation**

Nicki Minaj might have wowed them with the raunchy video to
her song "Anaconda", but an 11-year-old girl won the internet
with her pure dance interpretation of the song. Taylor and her
choreographer, Laurence Kaiwai, were filmed dancing along to the
hit track at Edmonton's KORE dance studio. The studio crowd
seem to enjoy it, but as soon as it was uploaded to YouTube, it
went viral. Millions agreed that Taylor had nailed it and her star
kept rising. She was invited on the *Ellen DeGeneres Show*
and continued to upload amazing dances.

http://y2u.be/pIZphVSrR-0

RESCUE CAT

The hero cat that sees off a vicious dog

All that his parents knew was that their four-year-old son had been attacked by a dog. It wasn't until they viewed the security-camera footage that the whole extraordinary story emerged. Little Jeremy Triantafilo was pedalling his tricycle around the front yard when he was pounced on by a vicious neighbour's dog that had escaped its leash. Suddenly, out of nowhere, a flash of black appears, bundles the dog off the boy and then chases the hound away. That flash was none other than Tara, the family cat. "The cat saved me," Jeremy told a local paper. " My kitty's a hero."

http://y2u.be/LSG_wBiTEE8S

A HAPPY SWIFTMAS TO ALL

The remarkable Taylor Swift makes Christmas special for fans with personalized presents

A near-tidal wave threatened America at Christmas 2014 when hundreds of teenage girls cried gallons of tears after receiving presents from singer Taylor Swift. Cynicism aside, this video documents the pop star's unprecedented acts of kindness, which she refers to as "Swiftmas". It shows Taylor wrapping up personalised presents for selected fans, and gifts being opened with squealing gratitude. In one case, Taylor even drives miles to personally deliver presents to a fan and her son. Many celebrities repeat how much their fans mean to them, but few give this kind of time and effort to making them feel special.

http://y2u.be/j3yyF31jbKo

THE MID-AIR *CIRCLE OF LIFE*

A cappella on the airways with the cast of *The Lion King*

You've just fastened your seatbelt, checked your phone is switched off, kicked off your shoes and sat back ready for your flight. What you least expect is to be given a private performance by the professional cast of *The Lion King*. That's exactly what happened to passengers on Flight 097 from Brisbane to Sydney, who were treated to a full-scale rendition of "The Circle of Life". In fine voice, the performers from *The Lion King* Australia go full throttle with a capella harmonies and handclaps galore. It certainly beats sitting next to the screaming child.

http://y2u.be/wgSLxl1oAwA

MEAT THE NEIGHBOURS

A prankster is out looking for trouble – or is he?

"You want beef?" Maybe it's not as common a phrase in Britain as in the States, but we get the idea. It means "You want to make something of it?" or "You want to fight me?" BigDawsTv, a YouTube prankster, went around his local streets asking people if they wanted beef and it's surprising how many were willing to take him up on it. Perhaps equally surprising is how many of them were willing to see the funny side when he revealed the ground beef he'd taped to the inside of his shirt.

http://y2u.be/tfZa1I8lxDo

PRICKLY EATER

The YouTube eating hero takes on his daftest challenge yet

Of course, he doesn't eat a cactus. No. He eats *two* cacti! The
LA Beast (real name Kevin Strahle) has form for this kind of
thing. He is a professional competitive eater with a seemingly
masochistic passion for the most excruciating challenges. They
include eating 36 eggs (with the shell), drinking a gallon of
Tabasco hot sauce and shaving his beard with wax strips. But
none come close to the pain of the cactus. There is also a video
of the aftermath if you like to see a man suffer.

http://y2u.be/d4KPWOUkbw8

ICE BUCKET CHALLENGED

**The best and funniest fails from the
great Ice Bucket Challenge**

The Ice Bucket Challenge was all over 2014, and anyone with a
camera filmed themselves being doused with freezing cold water
in aid of the ALS charity. Even the great and good were persuaded
to join in. Search for "Celebrities ALS Ice Bucket Challenge" and
you'll find everyone from Miley Cyrus to Selena Gomez to David
Beckham getting a cold soaking for charity. This video is far
funnier, though: the Ice Bucket fails. A whole lot can go wrong
when idiots, buckets and water come together and the great thing
about the challenge is that there is always a camera running!

http://y2u.be/uCromp-kIUU

THE CAT THAT GOT THE CREAM – AND STILL SCOWLS

Here is Grumpy Cat – she's not really grumpy and that isn't her real name

Her real name is Tadar Sauce, but everyone calls her Grumpy Cat and she is the most famous real live cat in the world. Grumpy Cat was only six months old in September 2012 when her photos first went viral online. Now she has a million Facebook friends, 30 million views on her YouTube videos and is soon to star in her own blockbuster film. So what's she got to be grumpy about? Poor Tadar was just born with a grumpy face, a loveable grumpy face that now adorns T-shirts and Christmas cards.

http://y2u.be/INscMGmhmX4

THE DOG TEASER

Magician uses disappearing dog treats as the ultimate dog tease

We've all had fun teasing our four-legged friends, even if it's just pretending to throw a stick and watching them scurry off towards the horizon. Magician Jose Ahonen is a dog teaser in a class of his own. He offers them a dog treat under their very noses, but before they get a chance to snap it up, he makes it vanish. The dogs' reactions are priceless. Desperately looking around, even nature's own detectives are bemused and befuddled by a sleight of hand. Dog lovers can rest easy: we are assured that all participants were soon rewarded with enough treats to compensate.

http://y2u.be/VEQXeLjY9ak

A CORPORATE VIDEO THAT ISN'T DULL!

A clever and hilarious parody of business jargon and corporate nonsense

This is a real advert for a real company and it's a piece of genius. IT company Risual have ripped the corporate video apart and put it back in a hilarious way. Despite claiming to have a "S**t ton of clients" and to be "the winners of every award for everything ever", the company still throws the kitchen sink at the ad in a brilliant parody of business speak and aspirational jargon. They cleverly subvert the IT stereotype and, in the final logo run, dig up every Windows and Word Art cliché ever seen.

http://y2u.be/_IHa-Dnh35c

BEASTIE MUPPETS

The Muppets meet the Beastie Boys in an awesome mash-up

Wondering what to search for on YouTube? The answer is always: try the Muppets. You'll come up with something special, although perhaps not always as brilliant as this. The clip is a mash-up, rather than a bona-fide Muppets video, but it won't fail to raise a smile. This is the Muppets as the Beastie Boys with the Swedish Chef, Animal and Beaker taking the microphone in the place of Ad Rock, Mike D and the late MCA in their classic rap hit "So What'cha Want".

http://y2u.be/kq-VNCGBDRU

HOW TO HANDLE THE JOB INTERVIEW

Actors act out a job interview – as imagined by kids

Kid Snippets is a series of comedy sketches where adults act out children's dialogue in as realistic a way as possible. This "Job Interview" is a choice episode. It is fascinating to see how toddlers view the world of work and how they imagine an interview situation panning out, but mostly it is very funny and pretty sweet. Does the young fella get the job? You'll have to watch to the end to find out – but there is an intriguing twist. If you like this, there are plenty more episodes: "Band Practice" is another gem.

http://y2u.be/fMX-07Lu6zM

DOGGY STYLE

A high-energy, dog's-eye view of a dash to the beach

The high-definition, lightweight GoPro camera has provided a number of YouTube hits, from extreme sports feats to stalking sharks. *Run Walter, RUN!* is one of the latest of them to go viral. It features a labrador harnessed with a a GoPro camera to capture a dog's-eye view. On a scorching day in Siracusa, Sicily, Walter is let off his leash. He runs from the house with only one aim – to get to the sea as quick as possible. Within 30 seconds, Walter has cleared gates, steps, rocks and bemused sunbathers on the beach to plunge into the Mediterranean for a refreshing swim.

http://y2u.be/UowkIRSDHfs

DOG BLASTS HORN

Impatient hound takes the wheel – and the horn

When Fern the boxer dog got left in the car on her own for too long, she found the ideal way to make her owners pay. Show them up on YouTube! The 18-month-old dog had been left in the car while her owner took in an art gallery in Broughty Ferry, near Dundee in Scotland. Fern was clever enough to know that simply barking at passers-by would not help matters at all, so she climbed in the driver's seat, leaned back and sounded the horn with her paw – repeatedly. Two million views online? That'll teach him not to leave me again!

http://y2u.be/y3xEPpwWGqk

CHANGE THE RECORD

Anyone else sick to death of hearing "Happy"?

Ready for a quick one? This is the kind of gag that YouTube executes brilliantly. Pharrell William's "Happy" song is a great track, but not everyone wants to hear it over and over and over again. That's why this perfect 12-second joke hits the nail dead on the head. I won't ruin it, but if you need the background details: the scene is from the classic film *It's A Wonderful Life*; the actress is Donna Reed and the record that is actually playing in the film is "Buffalo Gals", a popular American folksong.

http://y2u.be/3T-_Ao40CQ4

IRISH WEATHER REPORT

The Irish student's weather comment that went super-viral

When 18-year-old student Ruari McSorley from Derry was
interviewed by Ulster Television in Ireland about the recent
wave of bad weather, he thought his five minutes of fame might
spread around the locality. Instead, the A-level student found
his rich Northern Irish accent had become an overnight internet
sensation. "Honest to God... it went as far as Japan – overnight!
It's mad craic altogether," he is reported to have said. Meanwhile,
comments on his suggestion that "You wouldn't be long getting
frost bit" ranged from the smitten to the totally bemused.

http://y2u.be/O-m_BPYJG6M

BEST APRIL FOOL

Schoolteacher's phone rule backfires in superb prank

The best pranks are usually the simplest, and this is no exception. A teacher in Aquinas College, in Michigan in the US, had been enforcing his rule that students had to broadcast any calls that they received on speakerphone for the whole class to hear. However, his plan to humiliate them backfires on him spectacularly in this magnificently executed April Fool's prank. There is so much to admire here, from the great set up to the marvellous acting to the generous and good-humoured reaction of the victim.

http://y2u.be/R9rymEWJX38

KISS CAM DRAMA

**When her boyfriend won't play Kiss Cam,
she looks for someone else...**

Is this hilarious clip just too good to be true? Many suspect
this short drama that played out on the big screen at a New
York Knicks basketball match was faked, but so far no one has
admitted as much. An American sports tradition is the kiss
cam – a roving camera picks out a likely couple and, when they
appear on the big screen, they are supposed to kiss. This guy,
however, wasn't playing – hey, it happens sometimes. Except
his girlfriend wasn't going to be denied some lip action,
so she turns to the man sitting on the other side...

http://y2u.be/Qh0BwuxHRAg

DENTAL DREAMS

A trip to the dentist leaves a woman hilariously distraught

The post-dental anaesthetic clip is a common theme on YouTube. *David After Dentist* and *Unicorn After Wisdom Teeth* have been viewed millions of time and this clip starring Jayci Underwood is hot on their trail. Jayci is a little upset after coming round from the anaesthetic for the simple reason that she hasn't woken up looking like Nicki Minaj and isn't best friends with Ellen DeGeneres. We've all been there — haven't we? And you can also watch a lovely postscript to Jayci's fantasy rant if you search for *A Wisdom Tooth Dream Come True*.

http://y2u.be/idjo2fhLKDY

IT'LL NEVER CATCH ON

Furniture store catalogue ad is a brilliant MacBook parody

The furniture store IKEA prints around 200 million copies of its catalogue every year in 27 different languages. They are clearly not ready to move the whole operation online but have come up with a fabulous way of selling the concept. To launch the 2015 catalogue, IKEA produced this very funny parody of Apple's simplistic and dramatically voiced method of promoting new products. A suitably geeky presenter introduces the new catalogue as a revolutionary gadget. Then he continues to steal Apple's best lines as he explains how the bookbook has "tactile touch technology" and "328 high-definition pages" and how "the battery life is eternal". Spot on!

http://y2u.be/MOXQo7nURs0

LET IT HOWL

Puppy's amazing response to the hit from *Frozen*

We all know that little girls love the film *Frozen* and adore its song "Let It Go". But who knew it was a big hit in the pet world, too? Here's Oakley, the cutest Australian Shepherd puppy. He's enjoying his nap despite Charli XCX's "Boom Clap" blaring out of the car speakers. Then on comes "Let It Go" and Oakley's little ears perk up. In moments, he's up and ready for action, which, in his case, means howling along to his favourite song. When the track is switched again, Oakley's not interested. He's ready to settle back and dream of his life with Princess Anna.

http://y2u.be/ezz2NqvlORY

BROTHERLY LOVE

He doesn't want another sister and he doesn't care who knows it

It's a magic moment in a parent's life, revealing the gender of your new baby to your children. No wonder this family chose to celebrate the occasion with a cake. Cut the cake open, kids, and if the filling is pink, it's a girl; if it is blue, it's a boy. Sounds a good plan. The cake is cut and hey, it's pink. At this point, they all say how excited they are and tuck in. Er... not exactly. The two sisters seem happy enough, but the brother isn't having it at all. Cue the mightiest anti-girl rant and mother of all sulks.

http://y2u.be/VrAcV2ywnqc

THE FIGHTING IRISH

**Fabulously cross toddler tells off parents
for interrupting her song**

There's nothing a young child hates more than being laughed at
— especially when they are being deadly serious. The two-year-old
girl in this priceless clip is about to sing a song from Disney's
Frozen. Unfortunately, her parents have a fit of the giggles and
are distracting her from her imminent performance. She warns
them, but when they carry on giggling, obviously feels she has
to give them the telling-off of a lifetime. Choking themselves,
the naughty step, being sent to their room are all thrown at the
errant grown-ups in the cutest torrent of admonishment
— delivered in the finest Irish brogue.

http://y2u.be/zSyGRut7T0s

SHEENA MAKES IT CLEANER

Flatmate caught cleaning the house in his pants while dancing to 1980s hit

It's the morning after a Halloween party and there's a whole lot of cleaning to be done. There's nothing for it, but to get out the mop, put on some happy sounds and get to it – oh, and don't forget to strip down to your briefs too! Jimmy Pope is the almost naked guy in question, dancing and mopping away to Sheena Easton's 1980 hit "Morning Train (Nine to Five)" – until he realizes his flatmate has been filming him all the time. When this clip went viral in November 2014, Sheena pronounced Jimmy's performance as "adorable" and "Morning Train" briefly troubled the charts again.

http://y2u.be/cAs7qiQgi38

ANCHORS AWAY!

News presenters' under-the-table live reaction to earthquake

Those brave news reporters are always willing to put themselves in severe danger to bring us the latest news. The presenters on the news desk, however, don't appear to have the same dedication. An earthquake rumbled through Los Angeles in March 2014 just as news anchors Chris Schauble and Megan Henderson were delivering the headlines on TV station KTLA. At the first signs of the light earthquake, the pair shot below their glass table, only reappearing when the momentary shaking halted. Best of all is Chris's unwitting impersonation of YouTube's famous *Dramatic Chipmunk* as his eyes bug out on first sensing the quake.

http://y2u.be/KiB7ny52-xw

CLIPS DON'T LIE

University a cappella group's sensational mash-up of Shakira hits

Out of the Blue, an a cappella group made up of students at Oxford University, have tasted success before. They appeared on *Britain's Got Talent* in 2011 and reached the semi-finals with a cappella versions of songs such as Lady Gaga's "Poker Face" and Justin Timberlake's "SexyBack". However, even they were amazed at the reaction to the video of their mash-up of Shakira's hits. Doing their best impression of Shakira's own moves, they shook their stuff across the lawns and along the streets of Oxford, moving Shakira herself to tweet to her 26.2 million followers: "Hey @ooboxford, we LOVE your a capella Shak medley."

http://y2u.be/bRWVMPnByzo

CRY BABY

Devil baby scares the life out of New York City in an awesome prank

---

When this clip appeared in 2014, it was instantly acclaimed as one of the greatest ever pranks. A remote-controlled pram, complete with a realistic baby, cruises the streets of New York. When anyone foolish takes a closer look, the terrifying baby sits up and lets out an ear-piercing scream. Like some possessed infant, it is also capable of spewing out an unidentifiable liquid, giving the finger to a police car and uttering obscenities. The prank was part of a publicity campaign for *Devil's Due*, a now mostly forgotten horror film, but the clip continues to clock up hits.

http://y2u.be/yNz_9eSUMKg

HUMANS RULE!

Extreme sports highlights from the always excellent People Are Awesome

---

The People are Awesome productions are one of the most eagerly awaited videos on the whole of YouTube. Posted at the end of each year, the videos are a celebration of the physical capability of the human body and the unquenchable ambition of the human spirit. This takes the form of clips of people running, jumping, somersaulting, riding, throwing and generally performing a host of almost unbelievable feats. All expertly edited to an upbeat musical track – this year it's "Heroes (We Could Be)" by Alesso Featuring Tove Lo. Both mesmeric and inspiring to watch, it had racked up three million views within a month of being posted.

http://y2u.be/VWf8CXwPoqI

SKY-HIGH SELFIE

Taking a crazy selfie from the very top of a skyscraper

Vertigo sufferers, beware! This clip makes even the most level-headed of us take a firm grip on the arms of the chair. Don't get taken in by the casual banana-eating that appears to be taking place between a few friends. These kids have climbed to the very top of The Center, one of the tallest skyscrapers in Hong Kong to have their picnic. Standing precariously 346 metres (1,135ft) above the Hong Kong streets, Daniel Lau lifts his selfie stick. It's a wonderful view of the city, but you just want him to get down quickly and safely!

http://y2u.be/82SDk1kInvl

DIRT LUMPS?

Lip reading goes very wrong again with more priceless made-up quotes

Possibly this is even funnier if you are familiar with these American Football stars, but it's still pretty hilarious. The Bad Lip Reading people do what they say — they provide lip-reading interpretations of the sportsmen and coaches and get it very, very wrong. How else could they come out with such gems as "I once got a rake and I killed a snowman"? Or "You made a recipe and then you invented dirt lumps"? If you like this, there are plenty of other Bad Lip Reading videos, including fun takes on *The Hunger Games* and *Game of Thrones*.

http://y2u.be/OTRmyXX6ipU

PANDA PLAY

Panda cub Bao Bao experiences snow for the very first time

Sixteen-month-old Bao Bao is a female giant-panda cub who lives at the National Zoo in Washington DC. There are only around 2,000 giant pandas left alive in the world and a few hundred of them, like Bao Bao, survive in captivity. In her natural mountain habitat in China, she would experience cold and snowy winters, but it wasn't until January 2015 that she first witnessed the white stuff at the zoo. The excited Bao Bao ventured out to experience it for the very first time, tumbling down the hill in her outdoor enclosure, climbing trees and pouncing on her mother, Mei Xiang.

http://y2u.be/HQZ3-OD0ml0

SISTER ACT

A singing nun's breathtaking debut on *The Voice* in Italy

Sister Cristina Scuccia is a devout nun following the Ursuline order in Rome. She is also the reigning champion of the Italian version of *The Voice* and now a star in her home country. This clip is the first time most of the country saw Sister Scuccia. She wowed the judges with her performance of "No One" by Alicia Keys in this blind audition and shocked them again when they turned round to discover she was a nun. Cristina progressed through the competition singing "Livin' on a Prayer", "Flashdance – What a Feeling" and even duetting with Kylie – all available to view on YouTube.

http://y2u.be/TpaQYSd75Ak

FOLLOWING COMPLEX INSTRUCTIONS...

**An instructional video on making toast –
for the hard of thinking**

There is a wealth of really useful tutorials available on YouTube
from how to change a carburettor to how to perform brain
surgery. But seriously? *How to Make Toast From Bread*? It is
not even a joke – the woman giving the complex instructions
("take your slices of bread and put them in the toaster slots") is
completely serious (if somewhat lacking in on-screen charisma).
The Huffington Post went to far as to call it "the most pointless
video on YouTube". I haven't managed to find them, but
there are probably instructional videos on "how to breathe"
or "making a glass of water from water".

http://y2u.be/rJQpyIlV3-s

FUNKY PRESIDENT

Obama sings "Uptown Funk" in just about the coolest mash-up ever

You might love the original of this tune, but this version from a newcomer to the pop scene is so catchy you might actually prefer it! Barrackdubs have created a successful YouTube channel by editing together the smallest of snippets from President Barack Obama's speeches to make popular songs. Obama's "versions" of hits from Taylor Swift, Lady Gaga and Justin Timberlake were pretty popular and his "Get Lucky" garnered over 11 million views, but this take on "Uptown Funk" looks like being the biggest ever. Just to watch the President of the USA saying, "I'm too hot, hot damn!" is worth a minute of anyone's time.

http://y2u.be/wSnx4V_RewE

MAGICIANS VS VAMPIRES

The Hogwarts crew take on the Twilight gang in a fantasy dance-off

This video is like some fantastic dream you had but couldn't quite remember. How else would Harry, Hermione and Ron from *Harry Potter* face off against *Twilight*'s Bella, Edward and Jacob in the middle of a mystical wood? As the rivals meet head-on, it's time for a dance-off – with an umbrella-wielding Hagrid on the decks. Songwriting duo Scott & Brendo penned the catchy number to accompany this wilderness dance battle. Who wins this ultimate clash of magicians and vampires? You'll have to stick it out until the unlikely twist to find out!

http://y2u.be/_bcncbwlXR4

SQUEAK UP, MORGAN!

Honey-voiced Morgan Freeman in high-pitched helium experiment

Oscar-winning actor Morgan Freeman has one of the most distinctive voices on the planet. So calm, comforting and honey-coated are his vocal tones that he often provides voiceovers as God or an all-seeing narrator. So it's even funnier to see Morgan Freeman indulging in the old party trick of breathing in helium from a balloon in order to make his voice go squeaky. A word of warning: once the illusion is shattered, you might never see him in the same light again; it could ruin your enjoyment of schmaltzy nature films and credit card adverts forever.

http://y2u.be/DCpsusTta4w

CAN YOU HACK IT?

**Testing out some life hacks and bizarre hints
as posted on the internet**

A "life hack" is a trick, skill or technique that makes some aspect
of people's life that little bit easier. The internet is full of them, but
who knows which are truly useful and which are just myths. That's
just what the incredibly popular YouTube channel mental_floss
test in this entertaining, and occasionally useful, weekly series.
For instance, can you amplify laptop speakers with two halves
of a cardboard coffee cup? Can you open a beer with a phone
recharger? Or can you use tortilla chips as fire kindling? Those
and other life hacks are all put to the test in 10 minutes of fun.

http://y2u.be/3fQIYYZQBM4

CAN YOU HANDLE THE TRUTH?

A film trailer for *Lord of the Rings* that tells it like it is

The Screen Junkies channel run the Honest Trailers series, presenting trailers that tell the truth about famous films. With the classic baritone voiceover used in so many blockbuster films, they deliver an amusing and wry, if totally cynical, overview — trashing the acting, direction, special effects, merchandising and especially the sequels of your favourite films. This one takes aim at the *Lord of the Rings* series of films but there are no sacred cows — *Skyfall*, *Game of Thrones*, *The Lego Movie*, even classics like *Ghostbusters* and *Star Wars* — all are dismissed with the same caustic humour.

http://y2u.be/AOIi9SjJvgU

COP SHAKES IT OFF

Alone in his police car, a cop gets his funk on to Taylor Swift

Lip-synching is one of YouTubers' favourite pastimes, but you'll search long and hard to find a better one than this. The Dover Police Department in Delaware announced that they had been reviewing dashcam footage from their police vehicles and claimed to have found "something quite amusing". The footage featured a police officer named Jeff Davis, who has been with the department for 19 years. Alone in the car, he was singing along to Taylor Swift's "Shake It Off" in an extravagant, sometimes camp, magnificent style. Even Taylor herself was forced to retweet the video, saying, "LOLOLOLOL THE SASS." Whatever that means!

http://y2u.be/8XFBUM8dMqw

SMEAGOL HATES HALLOWEEN

When a hairless cat freaks out at owner's Halloween costume

This is wrong in so many ways. Firstly, you really shouldn't tease your pets as they are as worthy of respect as your fellow humans. Secondly, is it really fair naming your hairless sphynx cat Smeagol after the creepy creature in *Lord of the Rings*? And, finally, exactly when is it right for an (almost) naked man to put on a huge werewolf head? OK, that's the worthy stuff dealt with. Now sit back and watch an hugely entertaining short clip of an owner spooking the living daylights out of his cat. There's a Part Two as well if you like this kind of thing!

http://y2u.be/hZQd4u-A0KU

MR GARVEY CALLS THE REGISTER

The original hilarious sketch featuring the now famous Substitute Teacher

---

Keegan-Michael Key and Jordan Peele are the stars of the hit American comedy-sketch show that is broadcast on Comedy Central. Their sketches on YouTube are big hits and none bigger than this short sketch about a substitute teacher. Mr Garvey is a veteran of teaching in inner-city schools and is clearly having trouble with the culture of his new, mostly white, middle-class students. To begin with, he can't even manage to pronounce the names of some his students correctly. There are more Substitute Teacher sketches on YouTube and rumours that Mr Garvey is about to star in his own film.

http://y2u.be/Dd7FixvoKBw

TAKING THE PISTE

A day in the life journal of outrageous GoPro skiing stunts

Don't be fooled into thinking this is just another of those head-cam filmed show-off skiers videos. Well, it is – but Candide Thovex puts together the most entertaining GoPro experiences ever. His video takes us on a journey around the slopes of Val Blanc in France as he performs one outrageous trick after another; flipping, spinning and jumping clear over people on the piste below. He weaves through incredibly tight gaps between trees and doesn't even stop when the snow runs out, continuing to ski on grass and a rocky tunnel. Stay on for the amazing finale as Candide ends the video in hilarious style.

http://y2u.be/yKP7jQknGjs

PARALLEL WORLD

The World Record Tightest Parallel Park

Try this manoeuvre when you're faced with a tight parking space at the local supermarket car park. In front of a live audience at the 2015 Performance Car Show, British stunt driver Alastair Moffatt slid a Fiat 500 1.2 Cult into the narrowest of parallel parking spaces. Moffat's magnificent handbrake turn was made in a completely standard car with the exception of an enhanced steering wheel and pumped-up tyre pressures. Taking a space just 7.5cm (2.95in) longer than the car enabled Moffat to reclaim a world record that had been taken by a Chinese stunt driver. He bested the record by half a centimetre.

http://y2u.be/VSp1olKp_f0

SPARKLING REVENGE

Boy executes wicked glitter bomb revenge on his nosey dad

This clip was so popular that the company selling the "glitter bombs" were overwhelmed with pranksters wanting to spring a sparkling surprise on their friends. The lad posting the clip said he was so sick of his father opening his mail that he decided to give him a surprise. The company in question supply tubes full of glitter with a spring-loaded device. So he ordered himself a tube and set his camera up ready for when his dad got nosey. It couldn't have worked better – the "glitter bomb" showers hundreds of shimmering pieces down on the man and his desk.

http://y2u.be/y0yjATpkDxM

CUPCAKE KID

Three-year-old argues like a pro

He's three years old — and as cute as a button — and he's got
every trick in the book. It's not exactly the UN, but Mateo is in
trouble for trying to sneak a cupcake and seems sure he can
argue his way out of it. "Linda, honey, honey, look, look at this,"
he pleads with his mum as he puts forward a case that, since
he'd already eaten lunch, a cake would surely suffice.
And he's ready to use his oratory skills to protect his
brother from punishment too: "But he's my little
Pa-Paps!" he says. A legal career beckons...

http://y2u.be/TP8RB7UZHKI

THE APPARENTLY KID

The over-earnest boy who won the internet's heart

The kid's a natural, they often say. But Noah Ritter really is. In a short local news interview at a county fair in Pennsylvania, five-year-old Noah makes it look like he's been at it all his short life, even though he (three times) reassures his interviewer that it's the first time he has been on live television. But what sealed his internet fame was his use of the word "apparently". Eight times it pops up in the one-minute interview — but on the US *Today Show* he admitted he was tired of saying the word "apparently", even confessing, "I don't know what it means."

http://y2u.be/rz5TGN7eUcM

OSTRICH DROPS THE BEAT!

The big bird gets into the groove

The ostrich has a reputation for putting its head in the sand, but now we know the truth: it just wasn't hearing the right tunes. This bird is more than willing to shake a tail feather when the beat kicks in. A typical piece of YouTube opportunism matched up this footage with a great soundtrack and a meme was born. Of course, what is really happening is that the male ostrich is performing a common courtship ritual – he will alternate his wing beats until he attracts a mate. But why ruin a good clip with wildlife facts!

http://y2u.be/6BNVKEaYOVs

HIP, HOP... SPLASH

A cool rapper takes an unscheduled swim...

His record company describe him as a "street cat", but rap star Presto Flo clearly lacks the balance of the feline. The hip-hop artist took an uncool dive when on a photo shoot in Clearwater, Florida. Presto was doing his gangsta poses on the seafront, when a strong gust of wind blew his cap seawards. Reaching out to grab his headwear, he stumbled backwards, and the next thing he knew he was heading for the drink. Poor old Presto landed on an oyster bed and cut his hands and legs, but that's what you get for living life on the edge.

http://y2u.be/c7eXj92qqbE

HOLE IN ONE

Builder drops in at the golf shop

Security cameras captured this gem in a golf shop. The still of the shop is broken by a tremendous kerfuffle – which we soon realize is the figure of Ryan falling through the ceiling. Ironically, Ryan had been upstairs fixing the wires to the camera. Now, Ryan is not alone. Working with him is his mate, Billy, who seems pretty unsurprised to see his friend lying in the rubble. "Hey, Ryan," says Billy. As the casual conversation continues with the addition of a ridiculous comment from a customer in the shop, a YouTube classic is born.

http://y2u.be/EXvT8QbEMfQ

GRANDMOTHER'S DAY

A goal-scoring footballer wins the hearts of grannies everywhere

Modern footballers get a bad press with all their posturing, diving and fake injuries. So let's salute Roma's Alessandro Florenzi. After scoring a goal against Cagliari, Florenzi didn't tear off his shirt or perform some over-rehearsed celebration. Instead, he headed for the stands. Those waiting to see which blonde beauty he was headed for were gobsmacked to find him pick out and hug an elderly lady in the crowd. It was Florenzi's 82-year-old grandmother, who was watching him play for the first ever time. Back on the pitch, Florenzi got a yellow card. These referees have no heart.

http://y2u.be/C-ERsWiD9CQ

YOU'RE FAT, YOU'RE FAT, FAT, FAT

Witty and catchy mash-up of over-heated daytime TV debate

Our children are becoming more obese by the year. Whose fault is it? Is it our responsibility? What can we do about it? On a debate on the ITV show *This Morning*, the ever charming Katie Hopkins and journalist Sonia Paulton nearly came to blows over the issue. As insults got more and more personal (it's available to view on YouTube), presenters Phillip Schofield and Holly Willoughby did their best to mediate, but it was left to master mash-up merchant Dave Wollacott to put the whole thing into perspective with his silly, hilarious and even catchy version.

http://y2u.be/Hjiw6gmO4qQ

PRETTY ANGRY POLLY

Parrot takes exception to theme from *Titanic*

Gentle music is meant to have a calming effect on animals, but we all have our limits. Kiki the parrot usually enjoys the music her owner plays along to on his violin. However, on this occasion, from the very opening notes of Celine Dion's "My Heart Will Go On" – the theme song from the film *Titanic* – it is clear something is ruffling Kiki's feathers. By the time our virtuoso violinist has joined in, she is positively apoplectic and forced to take action. Listen out, too, for her mocking words at the end of the incident – priceless!

http://y2u.be/R1XiT25JIXA

GIRL POW-AHHHHH!

French feminist makes a stand — and a fall

The fight for equal rights for women takes many forms and so
we should salute the efforts of the mademoiselle in this video.
She feels it is time to make a stand against er... well, against
the fact that it was just men (and not women) being nominated
to be filmed jumping into rivers to be posted on Facebook. All
power to her: why should gender make any difference to making
an ass of yourself? So, very cleverly, she does not just jump into
the water, she magnificently makes more of an ass of herself
than any of her male counterparts...

http://y2u.be/kt5UaPFiYLE

HEAD IN THE CLOUDS

Stunning footage of Grand Canyon Total Cloud Inversion

Visitors who had travelled to the Grand Canyon in December 2014 didn't get the wonderful view of the immense canyon they might have imagined. Instead, they were treated to a pretty awesome and rare weather phenomenon called a "total cloud inversion". The canyon looked like a huge witch's cauldron as swirling clouds gradually filled it to the brim. The total cloud inversion usually happens every few years and occurs when warm air is sandwiched by cool air from the top and from below. The spectacular sight occurs as clouds are trapped in the canyon by the relatively heavier, drier air.

http://y2u.be/zF8LUy1LJjs

HAVING A WHALE OF A TIME

There's a killer whale under the inflatable!

Eric Martin, his son Cody, and their friend were enjoying a trip in their inflatable boat in the waters around Southern California's Redondo Beach when they were approached by a pod of killer whales. The boat, measuring just 3 metres (10 feet), was dwarfed by the Orca whales, who came right up close to investigate. They come face to face with the trippers and even swim right under the inflatable. The whales were later identified as a "friendly" family group who had a reputation for approaching boats – but never one as small as this.

http://y2u.be/Uv7pqqbXwQl

THE LIVING AND JUMPING DEAD

Zombie chase game comes to life in parkour thriller

This video combines three YouTube favourites — games trailers, zombies and parkour — and comes up with a winner. This live-action short film is based on the game *Dying Light*, a survival video game, and does a fabulous job of bringing the excitement of the game to life. Shot on the rooftops of Cambridge, the trailer, like the game, is shot in a first-person perspective with a non-stop, parkour-style zombie chase. Well directed and exciting, the video was well received; it went viral instantly, with over a million views in its first 24 hours of being online.

http://y2u.be/4NUOjzbFj1g

iGIGGLES

Giggling "Apple Engineer" recounts the invention of the MacBook

Are you ready to watch this video on your new MacBook? If so, you might want to know how the revolutionary computer came into being. This Spanish "Apple engineer" spills the beans on the 2015 MacBook. And it's hilarious. The video is actually a subtitled clip of an old TV interview with Spanish comedian Juan Joya Borja, known as El Risitas, or The Giggles, for obvious reasons. The enthusiasm with which the YouTube have greeted the video has led many to believe it is the new *Downfall* — the subtitled Hitler meme that wouldn't go away.

http://y2u.be/KHZ8ek-6ccc

A WOMAN'S TOUCH

Fantastic FIFA-acclaimed goal by Irish footballer Stephanie Roche

Cristiano Ronaldo and Lionel Messi are not the first footballers to have their heads turned by an attractive blonde in a designer dress. But the woman who caught their eye at the Ballon d'Or awards ceremony in Zurich was award nominee Stephanie Roche. The fantastic goal she scored for Peamount against Wexford Youths in October 2013 had been nominated for the award for the best goal of the season, and she had become the first female to be named a finalist. Roche missed out on the award but was named runner-up. Shortly after, she signed a contract with professional US team Houston Dash.

http://y2u.be/qpBvBRn4juw

BLIND FAITH

I Trust You, Do You Trust Me? Hug Me – Social Experiment

"I am a Muslim. I am labelled as a terrorist. I trust you. Do you trust me? Give me a hug." Canadian Muslim Mustafa Mawla was taking part in the Blind Trust Project – a social experiment "to break down barriers and eliminate the fear and ignorance projected towards Muslims and Islam". He was filmed as he stood blindfolded with outstretched arms on a busy Toronto street. In these days of mistrust and suspicion, how would he fare? Would Mustafa be shunned or embraced by the people of Toronto? Two million people have already watched the surprising results of this intriguing video.

http://y2u.be/epdkdbMEh0c

WHAM BAM

**Teenage rap duo Bars & Melody
wow Cowell with anti-bullying song**

Although Bars and Melody (BAM for short) only came third in
the 2014 series of *Britain's Got Talent*, there is every sign that
they could end up as the de facto winners. This YouTube video
of their audition performance, in which Simon Cowell pressed
the legendary Golden Buzzer, has already racked up over 65
million views and they subsequently signed a record deal with
Cowell's label. Consisting of rapper Leondre Devries and singer
Charlie Lenehan, BAM performed a song based on Twista and
Faith Evans' "Hope", with Devries replacing the original verses
with ones protesting against bullying.

http://y2u.be/g3Rf5qDuq7M

GHOST CITY

Footage from the empty streets of a twenty-first-century city in China

There is something decidedly spooky about the city of Ordos in northern China. There are no creaking old buildings or rattling gates, for this is a sparkling modern city, but nevertheless, it is the biggest ghost town in the world. Built for over a million people to live and work in it, Ordos was to be the jewel of a booming Inner Mongolia. Unfortunately, this futuristic metropolis that rises out of the deserts of northern China, never took off. Only 2 percent of its buildings were ever inhabited; the rest has largely been empty or has been abandoned mid-construction.

http://y2u.be/0brcZTVde-I

JENGA FAIL

**Reporter checks out world record Jenga tower
– with interesting consequences...**

If this is for real, it's the best fail on YouTube – if it's fake, it's a brilliant prank. So either way, it's worth a couple of minutes of your time. It concerns a model of the Leaning Tower of Pisa made out of around 12,000 Jenga bricks. It looks great, if worryingly built in the middle of a busy university library. The would-be record breaker just has to wait a week for the appearance of the Guinness record-approving officials to seal his place in history. Plenty of time, then, to entertain reporters from the local television network...

http://y2u.be/3Y6Lbgs2g4A

MEAN STREETS

The much-discussed *10 Hours of Walking in NYC as a Woman* video

One of the YouTube stories of 2014, this shocking video simply showed a woman walking alone through the streets of New York City. Over ten hours, a secret camera filmed 24-year-old actress Shoshana B. Roberts walking through various neighbourhoods of the city. She remains straight-faced and silent as male strangers greet her, make comments on her personal appearance, and even walk alongside her for several minutes. It creates a powerful message on street harassment and has provoked debate and parodies as well as many copycat versions of walking in NYC as a gay man, a Jew, in a habib and others.

http://y2u.be/b1XGPvbWn0A

COW IN THE HOUSE

"Ooops, I let the cow in..." And so begins a beguiling six minutes

---

What begins as parental investigation turns into one of the cutest videos ever in this everyday tale of family life. Billie Jo Decker has discovered the family's calf in the house and there is only one way it could it have got there: her five-year-old daughter, Breanna, let it in. As the cute-as-a-button child tries to talk her way out of trouble, her mother keeps the camera rolling. What emerges is a special bond between Brenna and the young cow as she snuggles up to the surprise house guest. As her mother says, "That's is just too sweet."

http://y2u.be/M5H7uMq3mS8

WHEN I GROW UP...

**Star comedian Tim Minchan's life lessons
for students at his old university**

"I didn't make the bit of me that works hard, any more than I
made the bit of me that ate too much burgers instead of going
to lectures." As a former student at the University of Western
Australia, Tim Minchin, composer, lyricist, comedian, actor and
writer of the smash-hit musical *Matilda*, was invited to give
address at the university's graduation ceremony. His inspirational
ten-minute speech in which he offers up nine life lessons to the
students is full of the wit, intelligence and modesty we have
come to expect from this consummate performer.

http://y2u.be/yoEezZD71sc

HIT THE DECK

Marvel at the spellbinding talents of cardistry artists in Singapore

---

Skilful, dexterous and fascinating to watch, cardistry is a fast-growing art. While card magic uses the handling of playing cards as an illusionary art, cardists, or "flourishers", manipulate cards in order to put on a show of skill. Flourishing techniques include shuffles, one-handed cuts, armspreads, springs, shapes displays and any number of nimble-fingered twists and turns of the pack. This video features a sextet of cardistry artists in Singapore as they show off their fascinating and hypnotic ability to manipulate cards, but if you fancy learning some smooth moves yourself, check out the thevirts channel, which is full of fabulous tutorials.

http://y2u.be/w_M_aRtX-bA

SWEET DREAMS, KIDS

Liam Neeson reads a bedtime story

If you are looking for a bedtime story to help the kids settle down to sleep, then skip this one. However, if you want a good chuckle, it could be the perfect clip for you – especially if you are a fan of movie hero Liam Neeson. While on US chat-show *Jimmy Kimmel Live!*, Liam took time out to read the children's story *Five Little Monkeys*. The stern voiced Irishman would surely be perfect for the story of bed-jumping monkeys being told off by the doctor. It does seem that way, until the actor loses patience with the repetitive story...

http://y2u.be/IQZAUVOMoGk

RAPPY EVER AFTER

Two of Disney's prime princesses battle it out in a rhyming rap face-off

"Of course you're bitter, I'm the Number One star. Pumpkin carriage, perfect marriage; no one cares who you are." Cinderella gets straight to the point as she goes head to head in a rap battle with Belle. The Beast's beauty gives as good as she gets: "Your tale's as old as time, sets us back fifty years. Do your chores, clean the floors, 'til a man just appears?" Rap battles are all over YouTube, but this is a pretty neat example. It is witty, bitchy and smoothly performed by Buffy actress Sarah Michelle Gellar (Cinderella) and Whitney Avalon (Belle).

http://y2u.be/VeZXQf77hhk

SIGNED AND SEALED

The world is reimagined for the hard-of-hearing in a poignant prank

---

Some ads are just too good to ignore. To promote their video call centre for people with hearing problems, Samsung Turkey came up with a heart-warming stunt. Muharrem is an ordinary guy living in Istanbul who happens to have impaired hearing. As we watch him go about his daily routine, we see Muharrem surprised, and slightly bemused, to find strangers around him using sign language to communicate with him and make his day easier. When the set-up is revealed, Muharrem's reactions are priceless. If this doesn't bring a lump to your throat, you surely have no heart.

http://y2u.be/UrvaSqN76h4

KNUCKLE DOWN

What happens to your knuckles when you crack them?

Up in the Top 10 ways of irritating your parents is cracking your knuckles. They will tell you that you will dislocate your fingers or that you will end up with arthritis. This video tells you what is happening to your hands when you make the popping sound that drives everyone around you to distraction. And it compares the hands of a man who has cracked the knuckles on just one hand, all his life. Is it just a harmless habit or will you spend your later years in agony? I think you need to know...

http://y2u.be/n3IYmdy6d4Y

SQUEAK UP FOR BRITNEY

**Britney's classic – without the music,
but with the jumpsuit squeaks!**

They just won't leave Britney alone! YouTuber Mario Wienerroither
has made an art form out of musicless music videos, but his
execution of Britney Spears's "Oops!...I Did It Again" is surely his
finest 60 seconds yet. Wienerroither strips the beats and lyrics from
an uncut shot of Spears dancing around her Mars ship and inserts
some rather too realistic squeaks and creaks that emerge from
her famous bright red vinyl jumpsuit. If you enjoy this, have a look
at Wienerroither's other videos, including David Bowie and Mick
Jagger's "Dancing in the Street", and the Village People's "YMCA".

http://y2u.be/cm0evQaHIE4

THE SOUND OF SILENCE

A priceless parody of all those *For the First Time...* videos

---

YouTube videos have borne witness to quite a few miracle moments. Cameras have recorded the first seconds when, thanks to modern science, previously blind people have recovered their sight or those with hearing impediments have heard their first sounds. This is something equally or even more special. It features a father of four who has not heard silence for ten years. The cameras are there as, thanks to the latest technology, he is finally able to hear it again. Oh, and it contains a bad swear word, so best avoid this clip if that upsets you.

http://y2u.be/18kqcczy6MQ

MILKY COLA SLUDGE

Interesting experiment showing the result of mixing milk and cola

If you enjoyed the Coke-and-Mentos experiment, this might be up your street. This video shows what happens when you mix cola and milk and let it stand for five or six hours. As you will see, some pretty strange science stuff goes on, leaving you with an almost clear liquid and a few centimetres of browny sludge at the base of the bottle. Basically, the phosphoric acid contained in the cola strips away the protein molecules from the milk, this dense sludge sinks to the bottom, and the remaining liquid becomes lighter and floats on top.

http://y2u.be/NhofonPRrFM

HOUDINI-PUS

Amazing footage of an octopus's escape through the smallest of holes

---

The things you can learn on YouTube! Would you believe a huge octopus can squeeze itself through a small letterbox-size gap? Well, the proof is here in Chance Miller's amazing footage of an octopus escape through an unbelievably small hole on a boat sailing near the Chiswell Islands, Alaska. The octopus is nature's great escape artist. Its long tentacles can feel the way out and its complete lack of an internal skeleton means that once it has the only hard part – its beak – through, it can just pour the rest of its body through any gap.

http://y2u.be/9yHIsQhVxGM

THE OSCARS GO GAGA

Lady Gaga does *The Sound of Music* at the Oscars – what a star!

The Hollywood Hills were alive with the sound of music as Lady Gaga wowed the millions watching the 2015 Oscars. Eschewing her usual flamboyant outfits, Lady Gaga took the stage wearing a Swan Lake-esque gown (perhaps a nod to "girls in white dresses"?). The singer sang a medley of hits from the Academy Award-winning film *The Sound Of Music* to celebrate the its fiftieth anniversary. Her performance included "The Sound Of Music", "Climb Every Mountain", and "My Favourite Things". And, to cap it all, she was joined by the film's original star, Julie Andrews.

http://y2u.be/vdqYmSf6tiE

MEALS ON WHEELS

Panic in the car as a safari park lion opens the door!

"Keep your doors and windows closed at all times" read the signs at safari parks. We've seen the way those pesky monkeys swarm over any vehicle, just looking for a way in. However, it seems it's not the monkeys we needed to be worried about, it's the lions. This video, shot on a safari park in South Africa, shows a family excitedly taking snaps of a pride of lions. A curious lioness ambles over to cast an eye over the visitors then, suddenly, like a concrete-jungle carjacker, she opens the back passenger door. Cue panic amongst the humans...

http://y2u.be/yeaztQK9lf0

INSTANT FRIED SHRIMPS

You won't believe how they make these fried prawns in just seconds

---

If you see one of these for sale in the electrical-goods aisle at your local supermarket, I suggest you snap it up. Then you, too, could be making battered fried shrimp in three seconds flat. You don't need to speak Japanese to be amazed by this video (it is a commercial for a mobile-phone company, if you are interested). Just watch as the shrimp are blasted through an air tunnel of flour, egg and bread crumbs before hitting the flames and the plate. That looks like pretty tasty lshrimp tempura to me.

http://y2u.be/IkaIoH6Um60

PRETTY IN INK

In slow motion, the dispersal of coloured ink is a wonder to behold

---

The Slo Mo Guys – Gavin Free and Dan Gruchy – take a £100,000 high-speed camera to film hundreds of times slower than you can see with your own eyes. The most popular of their videos find them exploding a water melon with elastic bands, heading a football and trying to burst a giant water balloon. In this excellent edition, they squirt coloured ink into a tank of water and film the result at 1,000 frames per second. The slow motion replay of the ink spreading in the water is, as the title suggests, completely hypnotic.

http://y2u.be/gzkB574jivA

THICK AS A BRICK

Ireland's stupidest criminal attempts to break into a car...

The guy in this video achieved the kind of fame you don't want when he was labelled Ireland's stupidest criminal in 2015. He tried to break into a car by throwing a brick through the window. Unfortunately, things took a turn for the worse for the would-be thief. He was found lying in a pool of his own blood by the car's owner after it rebounded off the window and smashed into his own face. Gerry Brady, owner of the car, told the *Irish Independent*, "You should have heard the gardaí [Irish police] laughing when they saw the video. They were in stitches."

http://y2u.be/dxSTDTVNpK4

EMMA TELLS THE WORLD

Harry Potter girl's passionate UN speech on gender equality

"Who is this Harry Potter girl? What is she doing at the U.N.?" Actress Emma Watson, who played Hermione in the *Harry Potter* films, pre-empted the question that she assumed many would ask. The answer was that she was a United Nations Goodwill Ambassador for Women and she was there to speak up for the He For She campaign, which calls for men to support gender equality. Watson, who confessed she was extremely nervous, surprised many with a moving and emotional speech that is worth watching right through to the powerful parting message.

http://y2u.be/Q0Dg226G2Z8

COPY CAT

Anything a dog can do, a cat can do too...

Is it a cat that thinks it is a dog? A cat that thinks it can do whatever a dog does? Or a dog stuck in a cat's body? Whatever it is, it's a fun video watch. Lucy and Phoenix the Rottweilers line up on the floor ready to perform a trick. Next to them lies a cat named Didga. On the command, each of the dogs performs a perfect "Roll Over". Then it's Didga's turn. How good a copycat is she? We're about to find out.

http://y2u.be/a_MqiGb0Qzk

BUFFALO KISSES

Snog, feed or avoid? A country park encounter with an amorous buffalo

Buffalos – the oversized bulls common to the USA – aren't famous for their romantic spirit. They are, however, partial to a piece of bread. Caroline Walker Evans posted this video on YouTube and called it *Buffalo Kisses*. As she and a friend drove through a country park, a couple of buffalo shuffled alongside her car. She decided to feed one a piece of bread. The next thing she knows, Caroline has a big hairy face poking through the window and a huge tongue heading for her cheek. Was it looking for more bread – or could it be love?

http://y2u.be/HK4cjWvkml8

SPEED DATING

The blind date where the guys end up shutting their eyes in fear!

The guys in this clip, all aspiring actors, believe they're auditioning for a new dating show. They're a macho bunch and they have no qualms about taking a ride with their attractive blonde date behind the wheel of a brand-new Ford Mustang. One describes himself as a "ninja", another says, "I'm a very adventurous guy", and one of her dates even offers to drive and show her "what this thing can do". What they don't know is that their date is professional stunt driver Prestin Persson – and she is about to give them the ride of their life...

http://y2u.be/3Nyr1Ao7iZA

THE DRESS THAT DIVIDED THE WORLD

That dress — and why we saw it in different colours

The whole world was talking about the dress. For once, it wasn't a daring number that a celebrity had worn to an awards ceremony, but a photo of a dress a mother of the bride had sent to her daughter. When the bride and groom looked at the picture, they each saw the image differently. When they posted the image to social media, it divided the world. Some saw a blue-and-black dress, while others believed they were looking at a white-and-gold number. How could people see the same picture so differently? This video attempts to answer that question.

http://y2u.be/AskAQwOBvhc

PLAYPIT HOUSE

Honey, I'm home – but she doesn't know home is filled with plastic play balls!

Roman Atwood is a serial prankster. His YouTube channel is full of hilarious stunts and this is one of the favourites. While his wife was out at work, Roman ordered a truck full of plastic play balls and turned his house into a giant play pit. He spread over a quarter of a million balls over the floors, then proceeded to dive off the stair balcony into them. When he finds out his wife is on the way home, he prepares a special treat for when she opens the front door. If you enjoy it, check out an extended version on Plastic Ball Prank EXTRAS!!

http://y2u.be/7t0EtKIQxyo

LOVE ALL

12-year-old outplays tennis ace in gripping rally

Roger Federer is arguably the best tennis player in the history of the game. His opponents have searched high and low to find his weak spot — but always in vain. So it was a big surprise to see the great man undone by a stranger from the stands — even more surprising, it was a 12-year-old kid. During an exhibition match at Madison Square Garden, his opponent, Grigor Dimitrov, let the lad play a point against Federer. The boy doesn't flinch. He lures the Swiss legend to the net with a series of shots and then goes for the kill...

http://y2u.be/hU2jPw0mjaE

GUESS WHO'S COMING FOR DINNER?

A giant grizzly bear fights four wolves for a place at their dinner table

It's only a rotten old carcass, but for a pack of hungry wolves, it must have seemed like a banquet. The last thing they wanted was an uninvited guest turning up for supper — least of all a 320-kilogram (50-stone) grizzly bear. This footage of nature at its most raw is compelling but not horrific. The four wolves show no fear in trying to chase the mighty bear away from their food but, equally, the grizzly is ready to take them all on. Who wins? Watch to discover a conclusion as fascinating as the fight itself.

http://y2u.be/6rBBPKUpC4E

100 YEARS OF BEAUTY

Time lapse video that illustrates a century of make-up and hairstyle changes

---

In just one minute of time-lapse footage, a model is transformed by a team of hair and make-up artists into different looks over the span of 100 years. We see make-up and hair routines evolving from 1910 to 2010 as model Nina Carduner appears in everything from the pin-curls and bow lips of the early twentieth century to the moussed-up style of the 1980s, ending with today's natural waves. This video has more than 20 million views and the producers, Cut Video, have followed it up with similar one-minute films.

http://y2u.be/LOyVvpXRX6w

THE DISAPPEARING PETROL CAP

Working out which side the petrol cap is on proves a real problem for one driver

---

Some people don't need a prank to make them look foolish. This unfortunate woman is not the first driver to have driven into a petrol station and parked by a pump, only to find the petrol cap is on the other side of the car. And who wants to risk embarrassment by trying, and failing, to stretch the pump around the other side of the car? Better to get back in and drive round the other way. Only this time, that plan doesn't work. The cap is still on the other side. So she tries again and again and...

http://y2u.be/TfHUsP0CI0A

MUNCHKIN WORKS OUT

It's walkie time for adorable Munchkin, the Teddy Bear shih tzu

Now you might find this adorable or you might just think things have gone way too far. Munchkin is a shih tzu dog from South California. She is pretty sweet as it is, but dressed up in her Teddy Bear outfit, and appearing to walk standing up, she pushes the cuteness into the red zone. Munchkin the Teddy Bear made her name as an Instagram sensation but found no problem transferring her skills to YouTube. Here she is working out on the treadmill, and you can also find videos of her on the red carpet, on the beach and out sleighing.

http://y2u.be/mVmBL8B-In0

THE HAMSTER GETS IT

**The sweetest little hamster gets shot –
and pretends to be dead**

Bless YouTube for still being able to come up with videos like this!
It's just 16 seconds long but is almost guaranteed to put a smile
on your face. In the history of the site, we have seen talented cats
and dogs and chipmunks pulling dramatic faces but never a
hamster with acting skills like this. Some, among the 11 million
viewers who have viewed the clip, have contributed their own
names for the performing rodent, including Arnold Hamsternegger
and Jean Claude Van Hamster. Can you do any better?

http://y2u.be/7nhll1UslDg

HAPPY ANNIVERSARY, YOUTUBE!

A superb montage of ten years of the best ever YouTube clips

On Valentine's Day, 2015 YouTube celebrated its tenth anniversary. The site has seen an incredible journey from a single upload to the 100 minutes that are posted every minute on the site today. This three-and-a-half minute clip features many of the best videos to appear on YouTube: from the original *Me At the Zoo* clip to *Charlie Bit My Finger*; and from *The Sneezing Baby Panda* to *The Evolution of Dance*. If you finish this book and are looking for more great clips, you could do worse than work your way through the playlist included in the first line of the video information.

http://y2u.be/wPd0MumNLbg

STRANGER THAN STRANGE

Ten photos of mysteries, conspiracies and strange phenomenon that defy explanation

---

If you like a conspiracy theory, you'll love this short video of ten photographs and film clips that have no apparent explanation. They range from a family picture in which a man in a space suit appears to be standing behind a little girl, to a mysterious old lady seen calmly taking photographs of the chaos surrounding John F. Kennedy's assassination, as well as pyramids on the moon, sea monsters and the bizarre behaviour of a soon-to-be-murdered woman. Along with the usual puerile comments below the clip, there are some interesting theories that attempt to explain the mysteries.

http://y2u.be/TU5rtGDaE9Y

THE SORRY CAT

**The cat that tries to say sorry –
then thinks better of it...**

There are so many good cat videos on YouTube and plenty of people watching them. This one has been viewed over seven million times! It's no wonder, as it has a little of everything; romance, pathos, violence and, of course, cats. Perhaps we identify with the kitty who seems desperate to apologize but continues to get the cold shoulder from his mate. He must have done something pretty bad to get a serious brush off like that. Keep watching, though, because the reason this is so popular is for the excellent and hilarious sting in the tail.

http://y2u.be/yNS7zzlzX-E

PIGS MIGHT SWIM

Swimming with pigs on a paradise beach

Swimming with dolphins is so last decade. Anyone who is anyone these days is swimming with pigs. The beaches and tropical waters of the Bahamas are known as the hang-out of film stars and pop singers, but lesser known are the fellas with whom they have to share the beach. A family of brown and pink pigs and piglets lie in the sun on the sandy white beaches and swim in the surf on Big Major Spot Island. Because they are so friendly and even swim out to greet incoming boats, locals have named the area Pig Beach.

http://y2u.be/BJuL-yK-l8g

STREET FIGHTIN' KANGAS

**In a quiet Australian suburb, two kangaroos
scrap it out "Thai boxing" style**

Street fighting is an ugly thing. It isn't fun, skilful or entertaining
to watch – unless it's two kangaroos having a set-to. Here we are
in a quiet suburban street with no one around apart from the two
marsupials trying to knock the doo-dah out of each other. There's
no drunken crowd, mates trying to help with a sneaky kick or
girlfriends shouting, "Leave him, Darren, he's not worth it."
As far as fights go, it's pretty clean, although there's a couple of
blows that look a bit below the pouch.

http://y2u.be/JyqJX7bU0Ws

BOOMERANG BRILLIANCE

Amazing trick shots from a boomerang master

It is not clear just who the guy in these South Korean adverts for Seoul Tourism is, but it is soon obvious that he is a master at his art. If this was in a superhero blockbuster, you would probably be shaking your head in disbelief at the accuracy with which he wields the boomerang. Using just a plastic version of the weapon, he manages to displace items from the head of someone standing 6 metres (20 feet) away, extinguish a candle and simultaneously burst a two separate balloons using two boomerangs. Is he still as good blindfolded? You better believe it...

http://y2u.be/UzaMDp3dgJc

SKYE'S NO LIMIT

BMX superstar Danny MacAskill returns with a scintillating ride on the Isle of Skye

BMX star Danny MacAskill's videos are always slick, beautifully filmed and full of incredible cycling feats. This is no exception, even though Danny swaps his usual urban playground for the breathtaking scenery of the Isle of Skye in his native country, Scotland. In an awesome journey, requiring all of the rider's great technical skills, Danny negotiates the jagged terrain, jumps rocks and rides knife-edge paths next to sheer cliff drops to become the first person to ride the island's Black Cuillin ridge, even climbing with his bike to the infamous "Inaccessible Pinnacle".

http://y2u.be/xQ_IQS3VKjA

JUMP FOR YOUR LIFE

Terrifying footage as a skydivers' plane is caught in a mid-air collision

Watch this in-flight footage of a terrifying mid-air collision 3,660 metres (12,000 feet) above Superior, Wisconsin. Panic sets in when the wings of the small plane burst into flames and the plane careers towards the ground. They had been hit by another plane whose skydivers were joining them in a formation jump. Fortunately, the divers were already on the verge of launching themselves out of the plane and soon the pilot joined them, too. Amazingly, there were no fatalities and only minor injuries as the pilot of the other aircraft managed to negotiate his way safely back to the runway.

http://y2u.be/7p6hqMnsLFY

OUT OF THIS WORLD

TV's Professor Brian Cox's experiment at the world's biggest vacuum chamber

---

TV scientist Professor Brian Cox travelled to the NASA Space Power Facility near Cleveland, Ohio, to test the laws of gravity. There in the world's biggest vacuum chamber, used to test spacecraft in space-like conditions, Cox raises a bowling ball and feathers above the ground and drops them simultaneously. With no air resistance, they seem to fall at the same rate but, as Professor Cox explains, they are not "falling" at all, but "at rest". As Einstein theorized, you wouldn't know if one of the objects is moving at all unless there is a "background".

http://y2u.be/E43-CfukEgs

BALLOON TUNE

1980s hit :99 Red Balloons" is played with red balloons

It takes a pretty unique cover song to stand out on YouTube these days. And they don't come much more unique than Toronto-based musician, Andrew Huang's version of Nena's 1980s hit "99 Red Balloons". Huang's cover of the catchy anti-nuclear ditty is played on… red balloons. His split-screen video shows Andrew and his balloon instruments, including bass, snare, melody and drums. Even Nena's vocals are recreated by a careful escape of air from a red balloon. The only criticism he seems to have received is for using just four red balloons. What happened to the other 95?

http://y2u.be/aZND9dApFKU

MINE'S BIGGER THAN YOURS

CCTV footage of an armed robber meeting his match

It's the moment every shop owner dreads — when a customer pulls a gun and demands the contents of the till. Except this shopkeeper in Pennsylvania, USA was prepared for just this situation. Unruffled by the intruder, he calmly reaches down and produces a gun of his own. His weapon certainly looks a whole lot more powerful than the air gun that the would-be thief was touting. The postscript to the video was that the robber was caught nearby after running into a nearby apartment. The local Police Chief said he was "one of the world's dumbest, and luckiest to be alive, criminals".

http://y2u.be/MLFEpaSAWVk

THE iMAGICIAN

**Amazing magician uses his iPad to do
more than just play Crossy Road**

The iGeneration are already pretty taken with their tablets
and now they can add magic to the list of iActivities. German
magician Simon Plerro performs his tricks with the aid of an
iPad and they are pretty stunning. Although he has already been
invited to perform at Apple stores and is the Angry Birds official
magician (who knew they had one?), this video features Simon's
big break as he demonstrates his iMagic on *The Ellen DeGeneres
Show* in the US. Using Apple's tablet along with traditional
sleight-of-hand techniques, he pours drinks into and out of the
tablet and wows his host with a pretty amazing selfie stunt.

http://y2u.be/b_xhSQGKxO4

A WINGSUIT AND A PRAYER

Take a helmet-cam flight through the narrowest of crevices with The Flying Cowboy

Just flying like an eagle in his wingsuit isn't enough for adrenaline junkie Marshall Miller. The man they call the "flying cowboy" was after a bigger buzz. He ventured to the Vermillion Cliffs near Minneapolis, USA. There, he leaps out of a helicopter, takes flight and heads along the Beehive Line, the narrowest of canyons. Like a real-life batman, he plunges through a rocky gap in which he can almost reach out and touch the sides. As Miller himself says on completing the flight, "That was pretty cool, eh?"

http://y2u.be/ev5JqIJvbiE

TOILET ROLL TUTORIAL

Hilarious dad's tutorial for teenagers that goes heavy on the sarcasm

Tutorials are one of the great things about YouTube. You can learn anything from changing a carburettor to making a soufflé. This tutorial, heavily laced with irony, is one of the funniest. The father of two teenagers, tired of finding they wouldn't listen to him, resorted to making a YouTube video. He produced a step-by-step guide to removing a used roll of toilet paper and replacing it with a full one. He adds that an advanced level would involve putting the empty toilet roll in the bin, but admits that may be "a step too far at the moment".

http://y2u.be/pNOY2EZuvTU

SELFIE PROPOSAL

**Awesome reaction to boyfriend who proposes
while pretending to take a selfie**

"Wha.. Oh, oh my God. Yeah. Are you serious right now? Is this for
real? Oh My God, oh my God! Yeeah!" YouTube does romance in
the best possible way in this short video of a marriage proposal
and the magnificent reaction it elicits. Lisa Holloway thought she
was posing for a selfie, but it was really her boyfriend's sneaky
way of filming his proposal. As he gets down on his knees and
pulls out the ring, the camera catches her hilarious and touching,
eye-stretching look and her words of total astonishment.

http://y2u.be/uH_Qu4ohdY0

3D? YOU BET!

Check out this awesome 3D video installation above a bar in a Vegas casino

---

The competition to entice gamblers into their rooms has led to some incredible displays in casinos. This video features an amazing feature at the SLS Hotel in Las Vegas, where those trying their luck are watched over by a giant three-dimensional golden face peering down on the casino floor. The incredible display is not a moving physical creation but a very clever optical illusion. The LED-laden structure measuring 9.75 metres (32 feet) long by 5.5 metres (18 feet) wide, and extending 1.2 metres (4 feet) deep, uses 2.1 million multicoloured LEDs. Its pixels are spaced at 6 millimetres (less than ¼ inch) to create a three-dimensional appearance when viewed from beneath.

http://y2u.be/EWvQ0cgQwXQ

THE CAT THAT DOESN'T GIVE A...

You can plead and beg as much as you want, but this cat is just BAD

The title of this video, *Gato malo*, translates as "Bad Cat", but this cold-hearted moggie is something else. He certainly doesn't look like he'll be curling up with you on the sofa any time soon. He's a real Bond villain of a cat; a pure evil pedigree gangster. OK, it's really just a 35-second clip of a cat knocking things off a coffee table – but it's the look he gives, the way he pauses to listen to his owner's heartfelt pleas to stop before continuing anyway and his pure "couldn't give a damn" attitude that makes it a winner.

http://y2u.be/UoUEQYjYgf4

SHAKE A TAIL FEATHER

**Has she gone? Right, it's time for this
owl to throw some shapes**

It's funny how some people just have to see a camera
to start performing, while others are happy to ignore a
photo opportunity. Well, this video proves that owls are no
different. Wildlife photographer Megan Lorenz has a GoPro
camera on her lawn filming a pair of burrowing owls. She has
hardly got in the car to leave when the owls appear to start
a dance-off, mugging it up in front of the camera. While one
doesn't seem that bothered, the other is ready to pull
some shapes and strut its stuff on the lawn.

http://y2u.be/SILvPVVAhBo

A MAN'S BEST FRIEND IS HIS ROBODOG

Introducing Spot, the electric-powered robot dog

You may have already seen BigDog, a gas-powered robot dog from the Boston Dynamic company. Now he has a little friend named Spot, who is electric-powered with a sensor head and super hydraulics. The 70-kilogram (160-pound) robot dog isn't the cutest mutt you've ever come across, but it can canter along next to a human, climb stairs and walk off-road. It can keep its balance when the meanest of people take a kick at it and, most impressively, it can walk next to BigDog without succumbing to the urge to sniff its bottom.

http://y2u.be/M8YjvHYbZ9w

PERFECT PLAYMATES

A heartwarming montage of surprising animal friendships

Warning. This video montage is so full of cute images it could send you into an ahhhhhh overload. This ad for Android software shows a succession of the most unlikely combinations of animals surprisingly getting along like BFFs. There are elephants and dogs, monkeys and horses, and even dogs and cats all playing together and pulling at your heartstrings. Now, it is unashamed sentimentality, but who doesn't want to watch a tiger nuzzling up to a bear, a rodent taking a ride on a tortoise's back, or a cat opening a door for a dog?

http://y2u.be/vnVuqfXohxc

FORWARD TO THE PAST

**Skateboard hero Tony Hawks get first
go on a futuristic Hoverboard**

This is so cool. The 1989 film *Back To the Future Part II* finds
Marty McFly (Michael J Fox) and his friend Emmett "Doc"
Brown (Christopher Lloyd) travelling to the year 2015, where,
among other technological advances, they see people flying
hoverboards. How fitting, then, that Lloyd is present when
skateboard whizz Tony Hawks and other luminaries get to be
the first to ride – or fly – this gravity-defying piece of wood
for real. If you want more information, look up *Tony Hawk Has
Something To Say About The New Hoverboard*.

http://y2u.be/HSheVhmcYLA

COLA COOK-UP

You'll never drink cola again when you see what it boils down to...

Not much is known about the CrazyRussianHacker except he has a fabulous 007-style Russian accent and a range of cool experiments. Here, he tries boiling a bottle of cola to reveal just what you are putting in your body along with the carbonated water. The result is shocking – a huge dollop of sugar and chemicals – looking even worse when he's burnt it to kingdom come! The CrazyRussianHacker also has some neat life hacks: check out his potato peeling with an electric drill or how to open a can without a tin opener.

http://y2u.be/LZp29Qeu8_U

CLIMBING NIAGARA

Climbing up a frozen Niagra Falls for the first ever time

The Niagara Falls are the world's largest flowing waterfalls.
People have gone over in barrels and tightrope-walked across
but, until January 2015, no one had ever climbed up the falls.
National Geographic's 2015 Adventurer of the Year, Will Gadd,
took advantage of the falls icing up to scale the frozen sections
up to the top along the line that separates Canada and the USA.
In a little over an hour, Will and his assistant, Sarah Hueniken,
climbed the 45 metres (150 feet), venturing close to the falling
water and even to the ice behind the falls themselves.

http://y2u.be/jU5i1WjRBhE

TAKE A BOW

Mind-blowing archery from a man who has re-discovered ancient shooting skills

---

Lars Andersen has been called "The Clint Eastwood of Archery". Forget the bow-and-arrow merchants of *Lord of the Rings* or *Robin Hood*, Anderson's archery skill is completely different – and awesome. The Dane studied the forgotten techniques of ancient master archers and, as a result, is a world-record holder in rapid-fire archery. His video is an astonishing mash-up of history lesson and stunt action, which sees him de-bunk Hollywood myths and pull off stunts like shooting three arrows in a second with pinpoint accuracy, shooting an in-flight arrow, or catching and returning an incoming arrow.

http://y2u.be/BEG-ly9tQGk

EYE PLAY THE PIANO

**An astonishing virtual reality piano that
is played with the blink of an eye**

The "universal piano" is a unique and amazing use of virtual
reality technology. Through wearing a special VR headset,
a user can select single notes or chords on the piano with a
pointed gaze and, through just a blink of the eye, they can play
them. Even the piano's soft-pedal effect can be invoked with
just a slight tilt of the head. It is, of course, a brilliant way of
enabling those with physical disabilities to play the piano, but
also opens up a world of new opportunites in the future.

http://y2u.be/VHXx7XTPULE

TEE TIME

**After an eight-year wait, Rory McIlroy
finally sinks a hole in one**

It has been achieved by amateurs, US Presidents, even Justin
Timberlake, but in all his games since turning professional in
2007, Northern Irishman Rory McIlroy had never enjoyed the
glory of a hole-in-one. He says he first sank an ace at the age of
nine and had holed a few first time in practice, but through all
his great tournament victories the holy grail of golf had eluded
him. Then he reached the tee at the 177-yard (162-metre),
par three fifteenth hole in the 2015 Abu Dhabi HSBC Golf
Championship. There his nine-iron shot bounced twice
before spinning into the cup.

http://y2u.be/Qy5YMVghzDY

NO ORDINARY JOE

**Impressive impressions from Joe Sugg,
the boy wonder of YouTube**

You are probably already aware of the ThatcherJoe channel, or at
least of its star performer, Joe Sugg. Zany, eccentric and good-
looking, the boyish 23-year-old has over three million subscribers
to his channel and a legion of fans he calls the Sugglets. One
of the biggest new stars of YouTube, Joe produces short videos
of challenges, pranks and impressions. This video is a good
example of his work. He's a pretty good impressionist with his
Elmo, Kermit, Shrek, Donkey and others being spot-on, but you'll
be won over by his charm, charisma and energy.

http://y2u.be/w42j-QWEqgY

FARTING ARCHY

**When Archy the horse lets rip, stand well back.
He really lets rip**

They say it's better out than in. And it's pretty obvious that's a sentiment that this horse will agree with. Yes, this is a farting video and a good one too – so if watching a horse fart itself into ecstasy isn't your cup of tea, then move on, there's nothing more to see here. This horse's name is Archy and the poor thing has an intestinal issue that makes it difficult for him to pass wind. So he lies on his back, has a bit of a wriggle and lets it all out in one long, marvellous fart.

http://y2u.be/jMyLOHdXPuc

PIRANHA FRENZY

Best not to dangle your big toe in this pool!

Those supposed scary films where people are fed to hungry piranhas are rubbish, aren't they? Well, take a look at this footage shot in a river in Brazil. Here, a seemingly tranquil river is suddenly turned into a bubbling bloodbath as someone decides to drop a piece of meat into a pool of the sharp-jawed little terrors. Apparently, piranhas do actually feed in a frenzy. They attack by literally taking a bite out of their victim, stripping an animal of its flesh within a matter of minutes and even taking bites out of each other in their mad haste.

http://y2u.be/9qf1Uew_HVs

CELLO WARS

The Piano Guys fight an exciting lightsaber duel — on cellos!

Originally posting YouTube videos in order to advertise a piano shop in Utah, USA, The Piano Guys struck a chord (sorry!) with thousands of viewers. Armed with a cello and a piano, the Guys say that their aim is to put a new spin on classic music and a classic spin on new music. By October 2014, The Piano Guys' YouTube channel had more than half a billion total video views and a handful of viral videos. This is one of the most fun — a *Star Wars* medley played by a Jedi Master and a Sith Lord with appearances from Darth Vader and Chewbacca.

http://y2u.be/BgAlQuqzl8o

IN THE DOGHOUSE – AGAIN

Denver the Guilty Dog is back in a Christmas confessional

Remember Denver the Guilty Dog who was shamefacedly caught having devoured a bag of cat treats? If you haven't seen it, it's on the suggestion panel on the right. If you have, you are bound to remember the yellow Labrador and be delighted to find her in trouble again. This time Denver – in collaboration with the cat – has been feeding on the foam ornaments from the Christmas tree. The red dye around the dog's mouth is a dead giveaway, but poor Denver gives that look that says, "OK, you got me! I did it. I'm weak and naughty. Please, please forgive me." And who wouldn't?

http://y2u.be/ogZWYn6qHSk

HOT LAVA, COLD DRINK

Ever wondered what happens when molten lava engulfs a cola can? Course you have...

This is just a short film of molten-hot flowing lava slowly engulfing an unopened can of cola. No, don't skip it – it's strangely fascinating. Perhaps it is the juxtaposition of nature in its raw state and the most famous commercial object in the world; maybe it's the miraculous high definition of the GoPro camera that captures such incredible detail; or it could just be the hypnotic effect of watching to see what happens to the can. Whatever, I'm not the only one; the video has had 21 million views and counting.

http://y2u.be/GaSjwAu3yrl

SMART-HOUND BUS

It's a smart dog that knows it's own way to the park — by bus!

Passengers on a Seattle bus have grown used to seeing an unaccompanied dog taking up one of the seats. It roams the aisles looking for a spare seat, hops up and happily sits looking out the window. When the bus reaches the park, up he gets and waits for the doors to open. The owner of the dog is usually a bus or two behind, having waited to finish his cigarette. Eclipse is a black Labrador/bull mastiff cross and seems to charm all the passengers he meets on the bus.

http://y2u.be/Bz4XEpK6INU

TRUE ROMANCE

True romance as flower girl and ring bearer boy marry 20 years later

It was the love story of the year. When Americans Brittney and Briggs Fussy got married at St Paul, Minnesota, it wasn't the first time the couple had walked down the aisle together. In 1995, she had been the flower girl and he was the ring bearer at a wedding between their families — they had walked to the front of the church arm in arm. Fifteen years later, she recognizes him in class and a romance blossoms. Fast forward another five years, and there they are dressed in their finery again — and this time they are the main act.

http://y2u.be/edVau9m6vHl

SHEET CHEAT

You didn't know you didn't know, but you'll be glad you know now...

"One of the biggest challenges you're going to face in life," begins Jill Cooper from LivingOnADime.com, "is how to fold a fitted sheet." One wonders what kind of charmed life Jill has led? Don't worry, it gets better. In fact, more than ten million people have viewed this helpful and practical video on sheet folding – and the comments prove it is undoubtedly a useful tip. The video itself is also proof of the fount of knowledge shared on YouTube, where you can find a tutorial on almost all of life's challenges.

http://y2u.be/_Z5k9nWcuFc

BEAUTY FROM CHAOS

Mousetraps and ping pong balls create an explosive New Year celebration

Stealing an idea from a science experiment on the chain reaction of nuclear physics, this incredible Pepsi stunt proves nothing except how beautiful ordered chaos can be. To celebrate the 2015 New Year, 2,014 mousetraps were armed and loaded with 2,015 ping-pong balls (eagle-eyed pedants might spot the advertising exaggeration, there are actually 1,650 mousetraps and 1,840 ping-pong balls). Triggered by a single ball, the result is a brilliant spectacle of flying balls and cartwheeling traps. The whole stunt took five hours to set up and took just 15 seconds from the first flying ball to the explosive conclusion.

http://y2u.be/-zX-gz1lRt0

BLINDFOLD LIMBO

Limbo dancing – without the bar. It's very funny

If you like a simple practical joke, you might just enjoy this clip from a humorous Norwegian TV show, set in Karl Johan's Gate in the centre of Oslo. The set-up here is brilliantly simple. After getting unsuspecting passers-by and shoppers to have a go at limbo dancing under a stick, the pranksters then suggest they try limboing while wearing a blindfold. As the foil begins leaning backwards, the duo disappear up the street with the bar. Who would guess that watching someone walking along while bent over backwards wearing a blindfold could be quite so amusing?

http://y2u.be/Vi41zAu4FfM

POOR GUMMY

How many times can a man shoot a giant gummy bear in the name of science?

This is a scientific experiment that is difficult to explain – or justify. This guy has taken a particular dislike to a gummy bear. Maybe it was that really, really irritating song that was a massive hit on YouTube. So, he takes a giant "world's largest" gummy bear and shoots it with a .22 rifle. Then he shoots it with a 12-gauge shotgun. Poor Gummy has a hole through him and part of his back missing, but the sadist then freezes him by submerging him in liquid nitrogen and repeats the 12-gauge test. Gummy doesn't come out of it well.

http://y2u.be/R2H0ZhO1NWI

HEART-WARMING HANDOUT

**A homeless man is given $100 in cash.
How will he spend it?**

This video by YouTube prankster Josh Paler Lin kicked up a real
storm when it went viral around Christmas 2014. In it, we see
Paler Lin giving $100 in cash to a random homeless man. He
then follows him with a hidden camera to see just how he spends
the money. As Paler Lin and many others guessed, the man heads
straight for a liquor (alcohol) store, but it was what happened
next that both surprised and shocked. The story found its way
to TV news bulletins around the world, but also found some
claiming the whole thing was staged.

http://y2u.be/AUBTAdl7zuY

ONCE MORE FROM THE TOP

BASE jumping from the highest skyscraper in the world

The Khalifa Tower (Burj Hkalifa), a skyscraper in Dubai, is the highest man-made structure in the world. It stands to reason that someone would jump off it. BASE jumpers Fred Fugen and Vince Reffet set a world record in 2014 when they leapt from a platform built above the top of the building, some 828 metres (2,716 feet 6 inches) from the ground. To make sure the video was impressive, they actually did the jump six times — in both free-fly mode and wingsuits — and circled the building one and a quarter times on the way down.

http://y2u.be/iD4qsWnjsNU

CHANGING BATTERIES

A sad but wonderful five-minute animation

YouTube is home to a fabulous collection of short films, especially animations. There are so many five- or ten-minute perfectly told stories that will make you laugh or cry and often both. This short film, *Changing Batteries*, has been around for a year or so, but keeps finding new viewers as people rave about it online. It tells the moving story of the relationship between an old lady and a robot. A word of warning, though: if you are easily moved to tears, it might be worth having a box of tissues nearby.

http://y2u.be/O_yVo3YOfqQ

CAMERON'S CONFERENCE RAP

Marvellous mash-up puts the Prime Minister on the mic

This video contains a rude word or two (not many), but if you can live with that it's very funny indeed. Michael Bollen and Steve Warlin, who together comprise Cassetteboy, have form. They were responsible for the wicked (in both senses!) *Nick Clegg says I'm Sorry* video and a series of other classic mash-ups. Using Enimen's "Lose Yourself" as a backing track, they brilliantly edit together a series of rhymes such as "I'm not saying it's not funny / It is for me, I've got loads of money" and somehow emerge with a coherent song. Ace work.

http://y2u.be/0YBumQHPAeU

RAPPING RADCLIFFE

Harry Potter star displays his rapping skills – and he nails it!

He's no longer Harry Potter, but actor Daniel Radcliffe still carries a touch of magic about him wherever he goes. Here he is on *The Tonight Show* in the US telling host Jimmy Fallon that he was inspired by Enimen and "had kind of an obsession with memorizing complicated, lyrically intricate and fast songs". We knew what was coming next... Daniel stood up and performed a word-perfect rendition of Blackalicious's "Alphabet Aerobics". If you are looking for more evidence of Mr Radcliffe's verbal dexterity, you could look up his performance of :The Elements Song" on *The Graham Norton Show*.

http://y2u.be/aKdV5FvXLuI

MOUTHFUL OF SAUCE

Italian-American chef finds "Worcestershire Sauce" a real mouthful

Pasquale Sciarappa's shirt may say, "No Sweat, No Sauce", but he manages to work up quite a sweat over his pronunciation of a certain British condiment. The 75-year-old Italian-American chef has been uploading his recipe videos to YouTube since 2008, but none have gone as viral as his charming attempts to pronounce the classic Worcestershire Sauce. His recipe for Stuffed Mushrooms required a dash of the sauce, but when he came to naming the special ingredient he faltered. Always a difficult word for a non-English speaker, Pasquale struggles to get his tongue around "Worcestershire" for over a minute before giving up.

http://y2u.be/YwTT8YQFJDQ

YOU'VE GOT TO BE JOKING

Record-breaking comedian fires off 32 jokes in a minute

"Went to buy a telescope... They saw me coming!", "Pollen count – that's a tough job!". OK, they may not all be funny, but you will surely laugh at one of Clive Greenaway's jokes. After all, he rattled off 32 of them in a minute. The professional Tommy Cooper impersonator officially broke the world record with 26 jokes at a show at in Suffolk, meeting the Guinness Records qualification of having a live audience and getting a reaction (if not a laugh) with every joke. The next evening he went on the BBC's *Newsnight* programme to better his effort – unofficially.

http://y2u.be/QF2JaMnLm-4

BOHEMIAN CARSODY

Aussie beauties send YouTube wild with in-car Queen singalong

Recreating the famous *Wayne's World* in-car singalong to Queen's hit "Bohemian Rhapsody" has been a long time meme on YouTube. But Australian female comedy trio SketchShe really nail it in this 2015 video. Sydney actresses Lana Kington, Madison Lloyd and Shae-Lee Shackleford throw themselves into the song in a tight performance full of humour (catch the cheesy literal mimes), flirtatiousness and energy. Their good looks and impressive lip-synching helped them racked up 17 million views in its first two weeks – a good effort but still a long way behind Queen's original. That has 130 million views!

http://y2u.be/aVx6cXf5Liw

JURASS-BRICK PARK

Great version of *Jurassic Park* with humour, authenticity and LEGO bricks

A father and his eight-year-old daughter put together this excellent three-minute LEGO version of the dinosaur film *Jurassic Park*. The stop-motion film recreates some and scary moments – including the attack of the velociraptors at the museum – just using LEGO bricks. OK, it helps that dad Paul Hollingsworth is a film editor and animation director with access to $100,000 worth of LEGO bricks and a small team of animation-industry professionals, but daughter Hailee makes sure it keeps its homemade charm and naive appeal.

http://y2u.be/5KNMYi5MDhE

DOMINO HOUSE PARTY

**A video which takes the falling domino theme
and goes somewhere very magical**

I can understand if you see the word "dominoes" and think,
"Maybe I'll skip this one", but this is pretty jaw-dropping. First
of all, it's a video to a cracking tune in A-Trak and Tommy Trash's
"Tuna Melt" and, secondly, it isn't a domino fall but a domino-
effect kinetic sculpture — so there! OK, there are dominoes, but
these critters climb staircases, turn on taps and unleash pool
balls, set off a feather-scattering fan and explode stick bombs.
And they kick off a marvellous multi-coloured tour through the
rooms of a two-storey house using collapsing toast, a paper
airplane, an unravelling necklace and an underwater submarine.

http://youtu.be/T8b-2biI8wU

CANINE CUDDLE

A distressed dog is comforted by his canine pal in this feelgood clip

---

What would be happening in a dog's nightmare? Do they dream of zombie dogs on the rampage? Failing their test at the obedience class? Or something as simple as the family getting a new cat? Jackson, a pretty wonderful-looking, one-year-old "Double Doodle" (the poster says that's half-goldendoodle and half-labradoodle) is having a bad dream involving a lot of scurrying actions. Fortunately, help is at hand in the form of his canine friend Laika. His reaction to his young pal's discomfort is heart-warming. As one comment says, we all need a Laika in our lives.

http://y2u.be/uTy_wUkWpkM

CLASSIC INTERPRETATION

**Simply brilliant funky sign language interpretation
of Swedish Eurovision song**

Magnus Carlsson's attempt to represent Sweden at the Eurovision
Song Contest in 2015 fell a little flat when his up-tempo song
was voted ninth out of 12 entries. His song, however, was the talk
of the nation, thanks to the performance of the sign-language
interpreter, Tommy Krångh. Tommy's interpretation of the song didn't
just communicate the lyrics to the hard of hearing, he communicated
the feel of the song too. "I get funky and just let go," the 48-year-old
told Swedish newspaper *Aftonbladet* after becoming an overnight
sensation. There are now calls for Tommy to interpret for Måns
Zelmerlöw, Sweden's winning entry for Eurovision.

http://y2u.be/SOOeBrQBPNc

LAMBORGHINI AVINGACRASH

**One of the world's most expensive cars goes
out of control on a London street**

If you owned a rare Lamborghini Aventador worth around
£300,000, would you risk it on the busy streets of London? The
700-horsepower Aventador is capable of accelerating from a
standstill to over 96km/h (60mph) in just 2.9 seconds. That can
be pretty useful on a racetrack, but is just asking for trouble
in the city's rush hour, where a potential prang is always just
around the corner. So to upmarket West London, where
the owner of this matt-black Aventador decides to put
his foot down on a quiet stretch of road...

http://y2u.be/kfS8iz2NaLE

NATURE'S LIGHT SHOW

Incredible time-lapse film of the Northern Lights

This beautiful time-lapse sequence was made by filmmaker Alexis Coram using 3,500 images shot over three nights in Alaska. The Northern Lights (scientific name: aurora borealis) are nature's own spectacular light show. The beautifully coloured lights that illuminate the sky are the result of collisions between electrically charged particles from the sun as they enter the earth's atmosphere. Carefully edited to a great soundtrack, Coram's breathtaking film shows the phenomenon in all its glory, bringing out not only the wonderful greens, yellows and pinks but also the fascinating movement of the lights.

http://y2u.be/x7M-uXMBjwg

HEY, OBAMA – WHY DON'T YOU JUST...

President Obama reads some of the mean things said about him on Twitter

---

Say what you like about American President Obama, but the guy certainly does have a sense of humour. A US chat show, *Jimmy Kimmel Live!*, has been running a series of films of celebrities reading aloud some of the nasty things said about them on Twitter. Hollywood's great and good have all appeared (they are generally very funny and available to view on YouTube), but few would have expected the most powerful man on Earth to join in the self-ribbing. Some are funny, some are mean, but the President takes them all in the best humour.

http://y2u.be/RDocnbkHjhl

BIG SISTER REVELATION

A little girl's surprise reaction to the news that she's going to be a big sister

It's a big moment for Dad. He's got to tell his three-year-old daughter, Kathryn, that she is soon to become a big sister. It's a stressful moment for a young child, so dad's prepared well. He's sat her down, he's bought her a book to help things along and he's got the camera rolling to record the moment for posterity. "You know why we got you this?" he asks her, pointing to the book. Then he unleashes the big news: "You're going to be a big sister!" No one, but no one, could predict what happens next...

http://y2u.be/hXg3QjtFReA

GAMER GRANNY GOES BALLISTIC!

Overexcited Granny gets revenge on British Gas on Grand Theft Auto

She uses some pretty foul language, but most people were able to excuse this granny as she gets immersed in a game of *Grand Theft Auto*. The senior citizen had just received an inflated gas bill from British Gas and used the game to vent her anger at the fuel suppliers. Off she goes on a hilarious killing spree of imaginary British Gas executives, shouting "Die, die, die" and swearing like a sailor as she blasts away with a sub-machine gun. I just hope she's calmed down by time the guy comes to read the meter.

http://y2u.be/HT3nrP4U6Nw

WET WEDDING

The best wedding video ever sees the whole party fall in a lake

Dan and Jackie Anderson really splashed out for their wedding in Minnesota, USA. When the family and close friends joined them for some photos before the wedding, the bride and groom discovered they weren't the only ones taking the plunge. As the 22-strong party lined up on a wooden dock, the structure gave way beneath their weight. A few bridesmaids managed to escape, but everyone else ended up submerged in the water. After collecting some unique wedding snaps, they had a quick towel-down and the ceremony went ahead as planned.

http://y2u.be/UaXaSfHuFu8

MELTING MOMENT

First-hand footage of the collapse of a massive iceberg arch

Wanda Stead and her husband's lovely boat trip out on the Bay of Exploits in Newfoundland was interrupted by the sudden collapse of an iceberg in the bay. Wanda was left fearing for her life as the arch in the iceberg suddenly started to crack, and within seconds, tons of ice began falling into the waters below. Wanda's video footage captures the dramatic disintegration of the iceberg, but also the panic as the large waves that formed started to approach their boat. She sounds pretty terrified as she shouts to her husband, "Run, Rick, go. Go!"

http://y2u.be/XEk5mNVc2Hk

DINNER FOR ONE... HAMSTER

A hamster eating tiny burritos – it's what YouTube was made for!

YouTube comedy group HelloDenizen combined two of the sites current favourites – miniature food and small rodents – and earned themselves a viral hit. Chef Farley Elliott meticulously chops vegetables and rolls them into tiny flour tortillas. He then takes his freshly prepared burritos over to the smallest of tables set up in a miniature restaurant. It's now dinner time for his little hamster friend who, to the chef's great relief, tucks into his haute cuisine fair with gusto. And that's it. That's how you create a video that's been viewed 10 million times!

http://y2u.be/JOCtdw9FG-s

TERMINAL BLUES

How bored do you have to be to lip-synch Celine Dion?

"What do you do when you are stuck at the Las Vegas Airport overnight?" asks Richard Dunn at the beginning of this video. His answer: "Shoot a music video on your iPhone. That's what." Instead of wallowing in his hopeless situation, Dunn filmed himself lip-synching Celine Dion's "All By Myself" in various heart-rending situations around the airport – from outside the women's toilets to the check-in desks to the X-ray tables. It is an hilarious night's work and we can be thankful that, for once, what happened in Vegas didn't stay in Vegas.

http://y2u.be/I9XLWrCi6DE

DANCING DIVA

The moment Brendan Jordan, the dancing diva, found the spotlight

"Every time I see a spotlight," 15-year-old Brendan Jordan said on TV, "there's this mode I snap into, and my inner superstar comes out!" Back in October 2014, Brendan was just another face in the crowd as a local television reporter covered the opening of a shopping mall in Las Vegas. Having elbowed his way to the front of the crowd, Brendan began to preen, pose, vogue and completely photobomb the shoot. America took the dancing diva to their hearts, as he was feted on chat shows, became an American Apparel model and an ambassador for an LGBT anti-bullying campaign.

http://y2u.be/yOOyfymbipg

RUSSIAN COFFEE

In the midst of violence and chaos, one man sits and sips his coffee

Every now and then, something crops up on YouTube which is intriguing, baffling and beyond explanation. This clip is titled *Just another day in Russia* and has around seven million views. It shows a terrifying moment when around 40 thugs, many of them masked and some possibly armed, storm a restaurant. They obviously target some customers, while others slip away as quickly as possible – except for one man. As all hell breaks loose around him, this one man sits quietly in the middle of the fracas and casually sips his coffee. It is all quite bizarre.

http://y2u.be/lmpLZalaaGU

A REAL BUZZ

Does this bumble bee really give a guy a high five?

Amid the pop videos, corporate ads and professional pranksters, there is still room on YouTube for the casual amateur to post something special. Now, you might not consider this footage of a bumble bee giving what is perceived to be a high-five to a young man as special, but it has been viewed one-and-a-half million times with over 8,000 thumbs up. While some killjoys have suggested that the bee is actually making a "back off" gesture, I'd prefer to think that the man's clear high spirits have won over an insect better known for its belligerence.

http://y2u.be/AgU4gXglEsg

CHANDELIER RE-IMAGINED

**Losing bet man reproduces Sia's viral
video in his own apartment**

The music video for Sia's single "Chandelier" was one of
the biggest YouTube hits of 2014. It featured 11-year-old
dancer Maddie Ziegler, who spins, kicks, twirls and leaps around in
a deserted apartment. The video was nominated for a Grammy and
received considerable critical acclaim. In less than a year, it has
been viewed a phenomenal 600 million times and, unsurprisingly,
it has inspired many parodies, including one by Hollywood star Jim
Carey. This, however, is my favourite. Apparently made as the result
of losing a football bet, the video shows Chuck Jose copying the
moves shot for shot in his own apartment.

http://y2u.be/5v24i9XTJq0

A ROARING SUCCESS

Getting a hug from a fully grown lion

Conservationist Valentin Gruener rescued Sirga, a lion cub, after she was driven out of her pride. Alone in the desert plains of Botswana, Africa, she would have faced certain death. He nursed her back to health and took her in to the Modisa Wildlife Project. Three years later, Sirga is still at the project and is learning to hunt for prey on her own in the hope to return her to the wild. She is now a fully grown 50-kilogram (110-pound) lioness, but as this amazing clip shows, she still recognizes and shows incredible affection for the man who saved her life.

http://y2u.be/sBw9V0Qz3I0